COME HOME TO *Yourself*

A Woman's Guide to Creating a Joy-Filled Life Through Self-Love

Dr. Linda Ann Westman
with Laura B. Fox

Open Spiral

First printing: 2025

ISBN 978-1-965101-04-9 (pbk.)
ISBN 978-1-965101-05-6 (hrdbk.)
ISBN 978-1-965101-06-3 (epub)
ISBN 978-1-965101-07-0 (Kindle)

Contact the author of this book at:
Linda Westman | lindawestman@yahoo.com | 406 876-4439

Contact the publisher at:
Open Spiral | editor@openspiralbooks.com

Book Cover and Interior Formatting by 100Covers

Dedication

To my parents, *Winnie* and *Elton Westman*
who provided an excellent foundation on which to build a life I could love.

For everyone who has felt unworthy or unloved:
Your presence matters.
You are meant to thrive.

May this book help you discover that a joy-filled life isn't a distant dream, but a state of being we can create here and now through gratitude, connection, and conscious focus on what brings joy.

CONTENTS

Acknowledgments

I feel tremendous gratitude for the encouragement and support I received from so many people.

The skill and patience of my co-writer, Laura B Fox was invaluable. Nitara Andersen, Madisen Hastings and Hanna Rausch kept me on track.

Flathead Valley Community College writing lab coach, Christie Harding, got me moving when I was stuck. Maggie Doherty's personal essay class was engaging and edifying. Kathy Dunnehoff's book *Hello Writer* and her monthly classes at Authors of the Flathead taught me effective writing habits.

I practiced writing and speaking skills with Glenn and Barbara Schiffman's Story Concert classes and at Toastmasters' meetings. The FVCC Library and Flathead County Library staff provided assistance and friendly smiles that kept me coming back to write.

Introduction
Hello Beautiful Soul!

I'm so glad you picked up this book. Whatever led you here—whether you're seeking more joy, deeper connection, or were led by a sense that there must be more to life than what you're experiencing now—trust that impulse. Your heart knows what it needs.

You might be wondering if it's really possible to create a joy-filled life, especially in times like these. I wondered the same thing for many years. But I'm here to tell you that not only is it possible, it's what we were born to do. It starts with caring for, appreciating, and deeply cherishing the life you are living now, however messy and imperfect that may be.

I know this is easier said than done! Believe me, if there was a magic wand that could instantly fill everyone with self-love, I would be dancing through life like Tinker Bell, waving it at everyone within reach.

Although we can't wave away our doubts and old hurts overnight, we can take small steps every day to treat ourselves with more kindness and understanding. That's why this book is packed with simple exercises that anyone can do. Some might feel a bit strange at first (just wait until we get to the mirror work!), but I promise you they work. I've seen these practices transform numerous lives—including mine!

Now, I want to be clear that filling your life with joy doesn't mean escaping reality. It's about learning to work with reality in a more loving, conscious way. It's about recognizing that you are a powerful creator, capable of shaping your experience of life moment by moment.

How, you might ask?

That's what this whole book is about! You will discover ways to tune into the wisdom of your body, clear away old emotional blocks, and open your heart to more love than you ever thought possible. You will have a front row seat to my personal journey as I learned who I really am and how to love myself through practicing these methods in my own life—sometimes gracefully, sometimes stumbling, but always moving forward.

Creating joy isn't like following a cooking recipe. It's more like learning to dance! You will need to find your own rhythm and style, though I'm happy to teach you some basic steps to get started. And when we begin to dance to the beat of our own heart's drumming, we become co-creators with God/All That Is.

Your joy-filled life is yours to create, so it's bound to look different from mine or anyone else's. Maybe your vision of bliss includes a cozy home filled with books and the smell of freshly baked bread. Or perhaps it's traveling the world with a backpack and a journal. You might find joy in raising a family, running a business that helps others, or finally writing that book that's been living in your heart—like I did. Maybe it's simply the ability to see love and beauty everywhere you look, in every corner of creation. Whatever lights you up inside—that's your personal piece of Heaven trying to manifest itself through you.

I've learned time and time again that what matters most isn't the big house or fancy clothes. It's our ability to feel comfortable and alive, full of appreciation, in our own skin. That, and having a sense of purpose, are what create the deepest feelings of happiness.

Finding joy isn't always going to be easy. You'll bump up against tender old wounds that still need healing, limiting beliefs that need examining, and habits that need changing. We're leaving the blame game behind and taking responsibility for our own lives. We're taking over the wheel and heading in the direction that gives us joy, happiness, and fulfillment.

No matter where you're starting from, and no matter what challenges you face, you can begin creating more joy in your life today. Even if you only have the tiniest spark of hope right now, that's enough to start with.

In this book, I'll share with you the practical tools and spiritual insights I've gathered over decades of my own journey and through working with clients in my chiropractic practice. You will find that you really can:

- Love and accept yourself exactly as you are
- Listen to the wisdom of your body
- Clear old thought patterns that keep you stuck

- See past limiting beliefs and change them
- Connect with your heart's deepest knowing
- Create positive changes in your life that last.

Most importantly, you will discover that you're not alone on this journey. There are so many of us learning to love ourselves better, to trust our inner guidance, and to create lives that we deeply enjoy. And when each of us does this work of creating more joy in the world, we contribute to raising the vibration of the entire planet.

Wherever you are on your path right now, know that you are exactly where you need to be. Keep your vision of a joy-filled life clear in your mind and heart as you read and do the practices in this book. Everything you need to create that vision is already within you. Sometimes we just need a little help remembering how to access it, and that's why I wrote this book!

If you can, I recommend finding a buddy to share this journey with you. Friends who enthusiastically support your efforts to grow can help you see obstacles you might otherwise miss–those little ways we tend to get in our own way without realizing it. Besides, there's nothing like having someone to celebrate with when you make a breakthrough! Plus, watching them grow alongside you is absolutely magical.

But don't worry if you're starting this journey solo. Many of us do. You might be surprised by how many kindred spirits appear in your life once you begin opening your heart, coming home to your body, and listening to the silences between your busy thoughts. (That's the work you will be doing in this book!)

The most important thing is simply to start.

Ready to begin?

With joy and appreciation,

Linda

Chapter One
A Mystery Worth Solving

It sounds like such a simple thing to experience love—all you have to do is to love yourself, or so they say. But for many, that's incredibly difficult. For most of us, it's uncomfortable to think about loving and being loved by anybody—least of all ourselves.

For much of my life, I didn't want to think about love. I didn't think I deserved it. And the idea of loving myself? "Oh, how selfish!" I thought.

As a little girl in Sunday School, I was taught that Jesus said to "love others as you love yourself," and the emphasis was always on others. But Jesus didn't say to love others more than yourself, or instead of yourself. He said to love them the same—the same amount of love, the same kind of love, the same in every way—because when

To love yourself means to see your value as a one-of-a-kind piece in the grand puzzle of creation.

you love anyone with the pure kind of love that Jesus talked about, it expands to everything, all of creation. If one of us is worthy of that kind of love, we all are.

I've been learning that loving myself more doesn't mean I love others less. In fact it's quite the opposite. The more I love myself, the more I see that we are all worthy of the same love. In fact, it's impossible to receive the love that's all around us if we don't first see ourselves as lovable.

To love yourself means to see your value as a one-of-a-kind piece in the grand puzzle of creation. It's recognizing that you matter, that you belong, that the world needs exactly who you are. When you love yourself this way, you cherish yourself and treat yourself with the same kindness and respect you'd offer a dear friend.

It has taken a long time for me to fully embrace loving myself—body, mind and heart. Now, before I leave this body, I want to share my story and tools so that you can experience self-love too.

My Heart Was Closed

If anyone had told me when I was a teenager that I would one day write a book about self-love, or any kind of love, I wouldn't have believed it. I had learned not to feel my feelings. Expressing them was out of the question.

I was 16 when the Beatles first appeared on The Ed Sullivan Show. It was a snowy February evening in 1964, and millions of Americans had tuned in to see the "British Invasion" that was causing such a ruckus all across the country. My dad had built our first TV set out of a Heath Kit, and the neighbors crowded into our living room to watch.

We don't have to keep lugging around the emotional baggage we have inherited.

As the four mop-topped young men in their matching suits began to sing "All My Loving," I felt a knot form in my stomach. Love was something I had steeled myself against, that struck a chord of fear in my body, I had no idea why.

While my parents and the neighbors stood transfixed by the Beatles' performance, I backed away from the screen. The lyrics, "Close your eyes and I'll kiss you, tomorrow I'll miss you" felt like an assault on the emotional walls I'd built. I couldn't bear it. I retreated to my bedroom, where I put on a Bach record. The mathematical precision of his fugues felt safe and predictable—devoid of the messy emotions the Beatles stirred up.

The Truth Behind my Story

I had always felt that my upbringing was pretty normal. So I was mighty confused when I realized in a college psychology class that I had all the characteristics of an adult child of an alcoholic. My parents only had a few drinks a year! When I asked my dad about alcohol in the family, he said, "Well Grandpa used to drink cough syrup sometimes." They were good Swedish Lutherans, those Dahlbergs and Westmans!

But despite my "normal" upbringing, I struggled with deep-seated feelings of unworthiness and a persistent sense that I didn't belong. I found myself constantly seeking approval, yet never feeling truly loved or accepted. This made relationships difficult. I didn't fall head over heels for someone until I was in college, but then I sabotaged the connection by visiting him at his Peace Corps assignment in West Africa after he told me not to come.

There were so many opportunities I walked away from without knowing why. It was as if success itself was threatening. Why did I keep repeating these self-destructive patterns? It felt like I was at war with myself. I so desperately wanted connection, but I kept pushing people away.

I was drawn to spiritual practices and healing modalities, always searching for something to fill the emptiness inside, but I didn't value myself enough to fully invest myself in making them work. I even changed my name for a few years, hoping it would lead to a new and improved me. For four years, four months and four days according to the legal papers, I was Regina Heigh Weir. But I couldn't fill the emptiness I was feeling by changing my name.

It took years of digging to find, feel, and uproot the fears and negative beliefs about myself that held me back. It was tricky because they weren't just mine. They didn't only come from traumatic events within my lifetime. Even in the womb, I tuned into the emotional state of my parents and my developing body responded to their anxieties.

My parents' fears about having their first child became doubts I carried about myself. They shaped my beliefs about my worth and my ability to be loved long before I could understand them. Even as my life unfolded in ways vastly different from my parents', I carried their emotional baggage as if it were my own.

I was born in 1947. Your challenges are bound to be very different from those of my generation. Student debt, climate anxiety, and social media are constant pressures that shape your daily life in ways my generation never experienced. The social fragmentation, sleep deprivation, difficulty concentrating, anxiety and other issues related to life in an increasingly digital world are well-documented. You might be struggling to earn a living working jobs that are here today, gone tomorrow, spending what should have been your savings on sky-high housing costs, lying awake at night wondering whether you'll ever achieve the financial stability your parents' generation enjoyed.

Although circumstances are different, the impact of inherited emotional patterns is the same. Whether you're a Baby Boomer, a Gen X, a Millennial, or part of Gen Z, we all carry the emotional legacy of our families and cultures. So much of what weighs us down was never ours to begin with. We inherit beliefs, fears, and patterns that may have made sense for our parents or grandparents but don't fit our current reality.

The thing is, we don't have to keep lugging around the emotional baggage we have inherited. We can set it down, open it up, and examine our old beliefs and fears. Once we understand where they came from, we can decide whether they still serve us or it's time to let them go. It's about recognizing that you are not defined by the fears and limitations of past generations. You are your own person, worthy of love simply because you exist. You are a part of the consciousness that makes up everything, All That Is, God.

This is key to self-love. I believe that coming to this planet in the first place was my soul's very first act of self-love in this

We're all unique—different experiences and activities light up our hearts in different ways.

lifetime. I'm grateful for this opportunity to correct things that may have gone wrong in a past life, like helping someone I may have hurt. I'm glad to be here at this time of transition, a time when feelings of joyful appreciation can elevate the emotional energies of the planet. I value the opportunity to experience the beauty of creation–including my own ability to create. I am grateful for the opportunity to grow through the challenges I have selected for myself. I believe that the same is true for you.

Creating a Joy-Filled Life

I was 37, studying for my Master of Psychology degree, when I experienced a profound revelation about love and joy. Through a poet named Harry Bromley, I discovered that deep fulfillment wasn't some distant dream—it was available right here in our everyday lives. His poetry spoke about love being the highest priority, the number one force in our lives. This idea moved me so deeply that I was inspired to paint a large pink #1 under the word "Love" on canvas.

This recognition that we could actively create lives filled with joy and meaning changed everything. I knew that I didn't have to wait for happiness to find me—I could consciously cultivate it in my daily life. This insight has been a guiding light for me ever since, leading me to explore what brings genuine joy and fulfillment to my life, and how to create more of it.

What about you?

It's up to each of us to find ways to create our own version of a joyful life, once we discover what it is that makes our hearts sing. We're all unique—different experiences and activities light up our hearts in different ways. Some find their joy in creative expression through music or art, others in athletic achievement or intellectual pursuits. Some discover it in nurturing relationships with family and friends, building communities, or developing their careers. There's no one-size-fits-all approach to joy—and that's the beauty of it.

So I ask you: What does your ideal joy-filled life look like? What activities make you lose track of time? What relationships nourish your soul? What work feels meaningful and energizing? These are the elements to focus on—the creative ways of expressing yourself that bring you alive: whether through music, sports, art, your family, friends, cherished partners, pets, home, career, or community. Give your time and energy to these sources of joy, and gradually release what doesn't contribute to your sense of aliveness and fulfillment.

In the rest of this book, we're going to explore how to identify unconscious patterns, how to release them when they're no longer useful, and how to cultivate the love-of-self that can fill our lives with joy. Because when you truly love yourself, you create a ripple effect that will change not just your life, but the lives of those around you. In the soup of all emotions on the planet, your joyful contribution raises the energy that all of us feel.

Practice: Tapping

Before we move on, I'd like to give you a simple yet powerful technique to help you start integrating what I've shared with you in this chapter. It's called tapping, and it's a wonderful way to connect your body and mind, helping to release old patterns and reinforce new, loving beliefs about yourself.

Here's how to do it:

1. Start by taking a few deep breaths to center yourself in the present moment.
2. Using your fingers, gently tap the side of your hand below your little finger while saying, "Even though I've carried others' emotional baggage, I deeply and completely love and accept myself."
3. Move to your eyebrow, tapping gently while saying, "I release what no longer serves me."
4. Tap the side of your eye, saying, "I am worthy of love, just as I am."
5. Under your eye, tap and say, "I choose to fill my own life with joy."
6. Tap under your nose, saying, "I release past generations' fears."
7. On your chin, tap and say, "I am open to loving myself fully."

8. Tap your collarbone and say, "I am creating a life filled with love and joy."

9. Tap under your armpits and say, "I feel safe being me."

10. Tap on the top of your head, saying "I am the love and beauty of life in full expression."

Repeat this sequence a few times until you feel a shift in your energy.

Tapping moves out emotions which were stuck in our bodies, releasing them, one layer at a time. Space then opens up for the pure light of creation to flow through our bodies. The resulting feeling of freedom and renewed energy is essentially what loving ourselves feels like.

With more creative power backing your thoughts and emotions, you will probably notice that what you think about manifests more quickly than usual. This also applies to thoughts and beliefs we have about our bodies. I have personally experienced the direct effect of unconscious thoughts upon my body.

I've learned to be mindful of what I am thinking, especially when my thoughts are amplified by strong feelings! For a simple example, I forgot to put my charger back into the computer case when I was packing up after working on this book one afternoon. I'm usually careful to put it away, telling myself, "Be careful, you don't want to lose this charger!"

When I couldn't find the charger the next time the computer's battery ran low, I started to panic. One of my old beliefs kicked in—that I'm always losing important things.

I was looking right at a charger lying on the table where I had last used it, but because my thoughts were screaming so loudly at me for losing the charger, my mind didn't register that this was it, right here in front of me. I thought it was for my iPad.

Instead of checking the end of the charger to make sure, I started searching online (quick, before the computer died!) and then went to ask at local stores when I couldn't find a fast delivery.

Finally, when I was in a calmer state of mind, I looked at the table again and there it was.

This is a literal example of how we see what our beliefs allow us to see, and our vision tends to be even narrower when emotions are heightened.

Fortunately, we have techniques like tapping to bring us into the present moment, where it's easier to see what's what and make conscious decisions!

I wonder if you can relate? Can you think of a similar situation where you missed seeing something that was right in front of you, simply because you believed it wouldn't be there?

How many beautiful, truly wonderful experiences in life escape our notice simply because we're busy being bent out of shape over something that may or may not even be real?

As you go through your day, try to notice moments when old, inherited beliefs pop up. How are the things you believe limiting your experience of what really is true?

When you notice that negative thoughts are running away with you, take a moment to do this quick tapping sequence.

With time and practice, you'll find it easier to stay focused on the love that is your birthright.

In the next chapter, we'll talk more about what self-love is, what it looks, smells, and tastes like, and how you can create more of it.

Chapter Two
What Self-Love Looks Like To You

In my early twenties, I briefly dated an elegant man who had a beautiful home filled with a magnificent art collection. We went to a sidewalk art fair one sunny afternoon. It didn't occur to me that any of the art on display could ever grace the bare walls of the tiny apartment I was renting on my entry-level salary, and I was content to simply browse.

Then a painting of a lively underwater scene caught my attention, and the man I was with noticed the impact it had on me. "Hey! You finally cracked a smile, Linda." At that time in my life, people were always accusing me of being too serious—I couldn't see why.

> Love, any kind of love, is connection. It's energy moving, like a prayer.

I was fascinated by the painting. It showed such a vibrant world under the waves. A hermit crab peeking out at an ephemeral jellyfish while a starfish seemed to dance by. Did I want it? Yes! But the price tag—it way beyond anything I had ever bought for myself that wasn't a practical necessity.

Before I knew what was happening, my date was paying the artist. He was buying the painting! My mind raced. For me? This can't be for me. We've just barely met. Nobody spends this much money on someone they hardly know. But he saw that I liked it! And now he was buying it!

I saw the painting each time I went to that man's house—which was only a few more times. It brought me joy to see it, and he joked that I was only seeing him for his art.

That was a funny thing to say, but I realized years later that in a way there was some truth to it. I admired this man because he was able to do something I hadn't yet found the gumption to do—buy stunning art just because he wanted it. The universe flung this truth in my face shortly after I had learned to scuba dive years later, and I saw a remarkably similar painting hanging in a gallery.

I wanted it. I had the money. I remembered vividly what had happened the last time I wanted something like this and held back. But still, a huge inner struggle ensued, and I almost didn't make the purchase. A big part of me believed that it would be a poor use of money to spend so much on something that wasn't a basic necessity. I had an unconscious belief at the time that if I cost too much money I wouldn't be loved. (I stopped eating when I was five years old because I worried that my parents would get rid of me for being too expensive.)

Fortunately, the self-love that had begun to blossom in my heart won out that day. Decades later, that painting is still one of my most cherished reminders that I am loved and that I can love—even myself.

Why was it so hard for me to buy something I wanted and could by now easily afford, while others made those kinds of purchases without a second thought? It didn't occur to me for a long time that my birth and early childhood experiences had led to the difficulties I had caring for myself and connecting with other people.

Love Is Connection

Paul Chek's definition of love as, "The flow of energy and information through empathic and compassionate connection to self or other" makes total sense to me. Love, any kind of love, is connection. It's energy moving, like a prayer, that moves from one sentient being to another. It flows and expands, and when it does it harmonizes, blends, and merges, showing us how we are all one. I visualize this as a blue light moving from person to person. I saw it vividly once at a ceremony where Dancing Bear led a group to create a medicine wheel at the foot of Chief Mountain, a sacred place for the Blackfoot Tribe.

So what does it mean to truly love yourself? It's funny how much easier it is to imagine the blue light of love moving from one person to another than it is to see it moving between the various parts of ourselves–mind to heart,
heart to body.

For me, self-compassion starts with nourishing my body and mind. It means feeding myself well and exercising to keep my body healthy. It's about allowing the divine spark within me to express itself freely and

When you truly love yourself, remarkable things become possible.

Nurture yourself and your intuitive abilities and over time you will begin to uncover hidden talents and passions.

joyfully. When I'm loving myself, I flow through life like a sparkling brook singing down a rocky hillside, effortlessly being who I am.

Self-compassion is also about taking responsibility for your own wellbeing. It's recognizing that no one else can make you happy or whole. Only you can do that for yourself. When you love yourself, you set healthy boundaries, speak your truth, and honor your needs without guilt or shame.

But perhaps most importantly, self-love is about acceptance. It's embracing each and every part of yourself. Your strengths and weaknesses. Your dark moments as well as the light you shine. When you look in the mirror, you have before you a human being deserving of kindness and respect. Your job is to learn and come to know that your worth is not tied to your accomplishments or what others think of you.

When you truly love yourself, remarkable things become possible. You start to attract healthier relationships because you no longer tolerate mistreatment or settle for less than you deserve. Life's challenges become hurdles you can jump, not walls that stop you. You're like a tree with deep roots. Storms may shake your branches, but they can't knock you down.

Nurture yourself and your intuitive abilities, gradually strengthening that connection with your heart, and over time you will begin to uncover hidden talents and passions. You might find yourself exploring new forms of expression like painting or singing. You may see new ways to solve problems in ways you hadn't considered before.

For me, creating a life I truly love has been quite an up and down journey, one where I'm still learning and growing. Although I can't say I always have ready access to that wellspring of joy within, I can already say that the rewards are well worth the effort.

We're Wired for Love

Love isn't just something that makes us feel good. It's actually critical to our health! Imagine your brain like a super-advanced smartphone. Just like your phone needs to connect to a network to function at its best, your brain thrives on connection with others and with Source.

When we connect with someone, we share our light, our love, even in small ways, and our brains release a cocktail of chemicals that improve all kinds of functions throughout our bodies. One of these chemicals is oxytocin, the "cuddle hormone." We usually hear about oxytocin in connection with childbirth, but it's not just for moms and newborn babies. We get a dose of oxytocin whenever we share a hug, a laugh, or even a smile with someone. It's like your brain's way of saying, "Yes! More of this, please."

Chronic loneliness, on the other hand, can actually be harmful to our health. When we're disconnected for too long, it's like our brain's battery starts to drain. Studies have shown that prolonged loneliness can be as bad for our health as smoking fifteen cigarettes a day. Yikes! Fortunately, just like you can charge your phone anywhere there's an outlet, you can "recharge" your brain's need for connection in many ways.

A Day in the Life

The difference between someone who loves themselves and someone who doesn't isn't always visible from the outside. It's more about how you experience and respond to the events of your day. Let me paint a picture of two different "days in the life," one lived with self-love, and one lived without it.

Without self-love, you might wake up already feeling behind and overwhelmed. The kids are arguing, the dog needs to be walked, and you've got a million things to do before you can even get to work. You skip breakfast, telling yourself you don't have time. At work, you say yes to every request, even when you're already swamped. You don't speak up in meetings, convinced your ideas aren't good enough.

Lunch is whatever you can grab quickly, eaten at your desk while you try to catch up on emails. By the time you get home, you're exhausted and irritable. Dinner is a rushed affair, and you snap at your partner over something small. You fall into bed feeling drained and unfulfilled, dreading the cycle starting all over again tomorrow.

Now, let's look at a day lived with self-love. The external circumstances haven't changed but your responses to them have changed. You still have all the same responsibilities and challenges. But your internal experience is different.

You wake up and take a deep breath, setting an intention to treat yourself with kindness today. The kids are still arguing, but you don't take it personally. You might not have time for a full breakfast, but you grab a piece of fruit, knowing that nourishing yourself matters.

No one ever scores a perfect "10" in every area. The goal is progress, not perfection.

At work, you still have a full plate, but you're able to prioritize what's truly important. You speak up in a meeting, not because you're certain your idea is brilliant, but because you know your perspective has value. Lunch might still be at your desk, but you take a moment to step away from your email and actually taste your food.

The evening is still hectic, but you find small moments of calm—maybe while stirring a pot on the stove or folding laundry. When you snap at your partner, you're able to take a breath and apologize, knowing that everyone has moments of frustration.

You go to bed tired, but with a sense of peace. Not because everything went perfectly, but because you navigated the day's challenges with compassion for yourself and others. Your circumstances may not have changed much, but, what's most important is that your ability to rise to the challenges has.

The person living with self-love isn't living a fairy-tale life. They have the same job, the same responsibilities, the same challenges as the person without self-love. But their experience of life is different. They move through their days with more resilience and inner calm. They're able to "chop wood, carry water." They do what needs to be done without it draining their spirit.

These two scenarios are like opposite ends of a seesaw, and most of us find ourselves teetering somewhere in the middle. Some days we might lean more toward one end, other days toward the other.

You've probably recognized bits of yourself in both pictures. Maybe you're great at setting boundaries but struggle with negative self-talk. Or perhaps you're good at nurturing others but find it hard to extend that same care to yourself. That's perfectly normal. We are all works in progress, learning to love ourselves a little more each day.

The key is to start small. Maybe it's taking three deep breaths before you get out of bed, or sending yourself a kind thought when you look in the mirror. It's about creating tiny pockets of self-love in your day, even when life is chaotic. Over time, these small acts can lead to profound shifts in how you experience your life–and you will find that your circumstances start to change too.

The Self-Love Spectrum

So where are you currently on the self-love spectrum? I created a quiz to help you figure it out.

I want you to approach these ten questions with openness and compassion. There are no right or wrong answers, or even final answers. The purpose of this quiz is not to pass judgment on yourself, but to show you where you are right now. This is just a snapshot you're taking of yourself standing at the starting line. So much can and will change as long as you are willing to do the work of being consciously aware of your thoughts. No one ever gets a perfect score—there is always work to do.

The nine statements ask you to rate yourself on a scale of 0 to 10, with 10 being total self-cherishing and 0 being complete dislike of self. After answering these, you will find open-ended questions inviting you to reflect and express yourself.

As you work through this book, you'll be learning new concepts, doing exercises, and hopefully, shifting your relationship with yourself. At any point during this process, you can come back to this quiz and take it again. You might be surprised at how your answers change, even subtly, as you progress.

When you've finished working through the entire book, take the quiz again. Compare your answers to when you started. Notice any shifts in how you describe yourself or handle challenges.

This before-and-after comparison can be incredibly powerful. It can show you, in black and white, how far you've come. It can highlight areas where you've grown and areas where you might want to focus more attention.

No one ever scores a perfect "10" in every area. The goal is progress, not perfection. Even small shifts can lead to big changes in how you feel about yourself and how you move through the world.

When you're ready, answer the questions as truthfully as you can. The more honest and thorough you are now, the more meaningful your results will be when you retake this quiz later.

Quiz: Self-Love Assessment

Rate each statement on a scale of 0 to 10, where 0 is "Strongly Disagree" and 10 is "Strongly Agree":

1. When I make a mistake, I treat myself with kindness and understanding.
2. I feel comfortable saying "no" to requests that don't align with my needs or values.
3. I regularly engage in activities that nurture my physical and mental health.
4. The thoughts I have about myself are mostly positive and encouraging.
5. I believe I deserve happiness regardless of what I accomplish.
6. I accept my body and personality, including the parts I'd like to improve.
7. I regularly take time to appreciate the good things in my life.
8. When faced with setbacks, I believe in my ability to be resourceful and move beyond them.
9. The people closest to me treat me with respect and support my wellbeing.
10. List three words you use to describe yourself.

I am ______________________________

I am ______________________________

I am ______________________________

Take a moment to review your answers. What do they reveal about your relationship with yourself? Are there any areas where you'd like to see improvement? How might your life be different if you showed yourself more love and compassion in these areas?

Write down your answers to these questions so you can look back on them later and celebrate the progress you will continue to make.

Self-Love Permeates Everything

When you love yourself, you become your own best friend. You speak to yourself with kindness and encouragement. You forgive yourself for mistakes because you see them for what they are—opportunities for growth. You make choices based on what truly nourishes your soul, not what you think you "should" do.

The shift in how you treat yourself ripples out into every aspect of your life. It's essential if you want to reduce stress, heal your relationship with money, become healthier, and enjoy your relationships with the people in your life.

Your relationships will improve because you're no longer seeking validation from others. You're secure in your own worth. Your work becomes more fulfilling because you're driven by genuine passion rather than a need to prove yourself. Even your physical health can improve, since you're more motivated to take care of a body you value, love and appreciate.

Chapter Three
Opportunity for Love Is All Around Us, All the Time

You might be wondering at this point, "Where does self-love come from? Is it something you're born with or something that happens to you? Can you just decide to start loving yourself one day?"

Something I often hear repeated is that "You can't love others until you love yourself first." I have learned that you can't give what you don't already have, but when I first encountered this idea, it left me feeling stuck. How could I learn to love myself if I didn't know what love felt like in the first place? People had love that they tried to share with me, but I was deathly afraid of love–and I didn't even know it!

As you start to treat yourself with love, you become more attuned to recognize love coming from others.

Understanding love when you've never allowed yourself to experience it is like trying to imagine the experience of snow when you've lived in Florida your whole life. Sure, you intellectually understand that snow is frozen water that falls from the sky, but until you've felt the soft crunch under your boots, seen your breath crystallize in the frigid air, or experienced the hush that falls over a snow-covered landscape, you don't really know snow.

We are made of love, so it's not something we need to create from scratch.

Love, especially self-love, can feel just as abstract if you've never allowed it in. Maybe you grew up in an environment where love was conditional or expressed in ways you didn't recognize. Maybe you've been hurt so many times that you've built walls to keep love out, even from yourself.

So how do we break this cycle? How do we learn to love ourselves if we don't know what love feels like?

The answer, I've found, is that we start small. We start with kindness, with compassion for the tiniest acts of self-care. These are the snowflakes that eventually accumulate into the deep, transformative snowfall of self-love.

It might begin with something as simple as speaking to yourself more gently when you make a mistake. Instead of harsh self-criticism, practice saying, "It's okay, everyone makes mistakes. What can I learn from this?" That's a snowflake of self-love.

Or maybe it's taking a moment to check in with yourself to honor your needs. Are you hungry? Tired? Stressed? Need a moment of quiet? Recognizing and meeting these needs, rather than pushing through and ignoring them is another snowflake.

It could be setting a boundary with someone who has been taking advantage of your time or energy. Standing up for yourself, even in a small way, is an act of self-love.

As you practice these small acts of kindness and respect toward yourself, you'll start to get a feel for what love is. You'll begin to recognize it, not just as an abstract concept, but as a lived experience. It's the small habits and acts of self-acceptance throughout our day that stack up to make a big difference over time.

You don't need to wait until you have a perfect, all-encompassing love for yourself before you can love others. It's not an all-or-nothing proposition. Every small act of self-love opens your heart a little more, making room for more love to flow in and out.

As you start to treat yourself with love, you become more attuned to recognize love coming from others. You might start to notice the small ways people in your life show they care. A friend who remembers how you like your coffee, a colleague who values your input, a stranger who holds the door for you. These were always there, but now you have the capacity to see and appreciate them.

So don't worry if self-love feels foreign or impossible right now. Start with one snowflake. Then add another. In time, you'll have created your own sparkling winter wonderland of love, starting right there in your own heart.

Love is Everywhere

We are made of love, so it's not something we need to create from scratch. We can focus it though, and direct it where we want it to go, using our thoughts. This has been done in religions all over the world since the beginning of time–we usually say that we are praying or sending blessings. Each time we bless another person, we are also blessed. This is ancient traditional wisdom, and it's something I've learned through personal experience. My process is simple—I like to inhale and send love from my heart to the other person.

Think of love like sunlight—it's always there, even on cloudy days. Sometimes we put up shades or close the curtains to protect ourselves from the sun's brilliance. But just like plants need sunlight to grow, we need love to thrive. And just as a plant will naturally grow toward the light, we naturally seek connection and love.

To really experience love, both for ourselves and others, we first need to open those curtains. We need to recognize and gently remove the barriers we've built out of fear or hurt that have been stopping the love from flowing in and warming our hearts.

Every great connection is built on a foundation of countless small interactions.

This is not as easy as it sounds. There's no magic pill you can take to make all the fear and pain go away. But once you start opening up, little by little, you find that baby steps do make a difference, and it usually gets easier to just keep going.

It's astounding how much love you can feel, even in the most ordinary moments, even when you're just starting out down this path. I don't mean romantic love or family love, though those are wonderful too. I'm talking about the love that exists in every interaction, every moment of connection.

Imagine you're standing in line at the post office. The line is moving slowly and maybe you're feeling a little impatient. But then you make eye contact with the person next to you. They smile and then you smile. In that brief moment, there's a spark of connection, of shared humanity, if you're open to it. That, my friend, is love.

Love Takes Practice

Practice doesn't have to be with other humans. it can be with your furry friends. One powerful experience for me was with a housemate's cat. I was sitting at the kitchen table. Her yellow tabby leaped up, rubbed his whiskers against my arms and pressed his forehead against mine. That instant when our foreheads touched—his forehead to my third eye—was a powerful time of feeling connected to another being. I had that now-familiar feeling that the same energies were operating through us. This was a connection that grew into love! What's not to love about a mellow, independent cat?

Sometimes, our attempts to connect can backfire spectacularly. Two incidents that happened in the same week taught me this lesson. The first happened at a small gathering in a local park. It was a close-knit group, meeting for a specific purpose. I had just met two new people and, in my excitement to foster connection, I invited them along. "The more the merrier!" I thought.

Oh, how wrong I was. One of them brought their dog, which turned out to be quite disruptive. I should have asked them to put the dog in their truck, but I froze. I felt helpless, just like that little three-year-old girl inside me who couldn't speak up. The group's energy shifted, and I could feel the others' discomfort. My attempt to bring people together had inadvertently created tension.

A similar thing happened with an online group. It was a small, established community, and I invited someone new to join a call. This disrupted the flow of the session, since orienting the new person took up valuable time. Again, my eagerness to include everyone had caused complications.

In both situations, my heart was in the right place. I have this deep, burning desire to bring people together, to ensure no one feels left out like I did for so much of my life. It's a beautiful gift, actually. And my childlike nature, my ability to approach the world with wonder and playfulness, is another gift. But like any gift, these need to be honed before we're able to use them appropriately.

It's easy to feel discouraged when our attempts at connection go awry. We might be tempted to withdraw, to stop trying. But that's not the answer. Each misstep is an opportunity to refine our approach. We're still learning, after all!

So how do we keep practicing? First, we need to forgive ourselves for our mistakes. Then, we can reflect on what went wrong and how we might handle it differently next time. Maybe I could have checked with the group leader before inviting new people. Perhaps I could have set clear boundaries about the dog. I will know better next time a situation like this arises.

Most importantly, we need to keep our hearts open. Yes, it can be scary to put ourselves out there again after a setback. But the alternative, closing ourselves off from connection, is far more painful in the long run.

Every great connection, every moment free of judgment, with unconditional love and belonging, is built on a foundation of countless small interactions, some awkward, some beautiful. It's all part of the journey. You have unique gifts that no one else can bring to the table. When you keep practicing, keep learning, keep growing and sharing your light, you free your true voice and feel safer and safer expressing your authentic self, your heart. The world needs your light, even if it takes you a while to figure out how best to shine it.

Put Up Your Antenna and Switch on Your Radio

Once you get familiar with what it's like to experience love, it gets easier to find. It's like switching on an internal radio, putting up your antenna, and tuning into a frequency that's been playing all along. Once you're aware of it, you start to feel it everywhere.

The barista who remembers your usual order? That's love. The neighbor who waves to you from her garden? That's love too.

I challenge you today: Open your heart, and be the love you've been looking for!

Even the tree that provides shade on a hot day is an expression of the love that permeates the whole world.

When you open yourself to receiving this love, these moments of connection, something miraculous happens. You start to fill up with it. It's like you're an empty vessel that's been slowly filling with this beautiful, life-giving energy. As you fill up, you naturally start to overflow. You begin to radiate that love back out into the world without even trying.

As you recognize and appreciate the love around you, you start to see yourself as part of that loving world. You realize that you, too, are worthy of that love. You start to treat yourself with the same kindness and appreciation you're noticing everywhere else.

And then—oh, it's so beautiful! You become a source of love yourself. You catch yourself smiling at a stranger passing you on the sidewalk, they smile in response, and then the next person they pass catches that lingering smile. Your kind words to a coworker having a bad day inspire her to be gentler with herself. It's a wonderful, ever-expanding cycle.

I get so excited about this because it's such a simple truth, yet it has the power to transform our entire experience of life. We don't have to wait for love to come to us. We don't have to achieve anything or become someone different to deserve love. All we need to do is open our eyes, put up our antennas, and tune into what we value, and then consciously connect with the love that's already here.

So I challenge you today: Open your heart, and be the love you've been looking for! I promise you, once you start looking for what delights you, you'll feel the love within you expanding, and you won't be able to help spreading that love to others.

Know that each of us is born with that essential spark of divine love. You can think of it as a pilot light that you can turn up any time through acts of self-care. Consciously choosing to get enough sleep, taking the time to eat healthy foods, and really seeing the beauty in everything around us are great ways to keep that flame burning. That small flame grows and becomes a powerful light that radiates from us wherever we go, warming and illuminating those around us, and kindling their inner flames too. This is how loving ourselves ultimately raises the vibration of mass consciousness and brings us closer to a joy-filled world for all.

You are learning to allow the love that already surrounds you to flow through you. Isn't that beautiful? You're part of this grand, cosmic flow of love. All you are learning is to open up and let it in.

It's Scary but So Worthwhile

I know what you might be thinking right now. "Linda, this all sounds beautiful, but it's scary. What if I open up and get hurt? What if I raise my antenna and only pick up static?"

I hear you. I've been there and sometimes I'm still there. Opening yourself up to love, even the everyday kind I'm talking about, takes real courage. It means lowering defenses you've probably had in place since childhood, maybe even since previous lifetimes. Those walls weren't built overnight, after all. And they weren't built without reason. They've protected you from very real pain.

Although your walls might keep out hurt, they also keep out joy, connection, and yes, love. It's like living in a fortress. Sure, you're safe, but you're also isolated.

Loving yourself means valuing and accepting yourself for who you are.

Yes, opening up feels vulnerable. But oh, it is so worth it. As you gradually open up, you'll start to build new experiences that counteract your fears. You'll find that most people respond positively to openness. You'll discover that you're stronger than you thought, able to handle moments of disappointment because they're outweighed by moments of connection.

It takes courage. But you have that courage within you. You've survived every difficult day you've faced so far, and that takes strength, doesn't it? Now you can use that strength not just to survive, but to thrive, to open yourself to the love that's been waiting for you all along.

As you start to recognize and appreciate these moments of connection, it will become more apparent that you really are a part of this web of love and support. It becomes easier to extend that same kindness and appreciation to yourself. This is where self-love begins to grow.

As Without, So Within

This chapter wouldn't be complete without addressing another kind of disconnection that's just as important—disconnection within ourselves. Love is connection, and while we might feel fragmented inside, like we're still figuring out who we are, we can love ourselves with all our confusing contradictions. We might spend years trying to understand our own mysteries. Why do we avoid doing things we say we want to do? Why do we react strongly to situations that we think shouldn't bother us? Even at times when it looks like a stranger is living our lives, we can still have compassion for ourselves. Each small moment of noticing and caring for ourselves becomes a step toward feeling more whole inside.

In our modern world, we tend to live from the neck up. We're so caught up in our thoughts, our to-do lists, our worries about the future or regrets about the past, that we forget we have bodies at all. We might go entire days without really feeling our feet on the ground or noticing the rise and fall of our breath.

This disconnection goes beyond just being "in our heads." Sometimes, due to past traumas or long-held beliefs about ourselves, we actually cut off awareness from parts of our bodies. I've seen this in my work with clients, and I've experienced it myself. Maybe you've had a traumatic experience with your right hand, so you unconsciously avoid using or even feeling that hand. Or perhaps you've internalized shame about your weight, so you disconnect from your stomach or your hips.

Emotionally, we might disconnect from certain feelings because they seem too overwhelming or because we were taught they were unacceptable. We might push down our anger, or numb ourselves to sadness, or even disconnect from joy because we're afraid it won't last.

All of this internal disconnection affects how we care for ourselves. When we push away parts of ourselves, it's like telling them "you don't matter." But we can start small, learning to listen to more of who we are. Our bodies and hearts, as well as our minds, carry important messages for us.

Learning where our stories come from allows us to see them through a lens of compassion.

They tell us when we need rest, when we're in danger, and even when we need certain foods that provide nutrition our bodies lack. Right now, your body might be trying to alert you to an opportunity for real happiness that you're leaving on the table!

When we find and reconnect to lost parts of ourselves, such as the fearful, wounded child that lives in all of us, we discover that they hold the keys to healing from old wounds and beliefs. Learning where our stories come from allows us to see them through a lens of compassion and find the power to change those stories. It's like giving ourselves a big hug from the inside out.

When I started to solve the mystery of how I had become the person I was, and I learned to see myself as a sacred human-spiritual being instead of as a strange person unworthy of love, I began to love myself.

It takes effort and patient practice to see ourselves for who we really are. Until we do, it's like we're looking at the world through glasses with cracked lenses that make everything seem fragmented. Every hurtful experience throughout our lives adds another crack. It's easy to forget that these cracked lenses aren't part of us. They aren't our actual eyes. We're so used to wearing them though, it's hard to take them off.

Dissolving the illusion of separation takes a sort of brazen curiosity to look deeply at ourselves. When you do, you will find that you are not alone. You are not unloved. You are a beautiful, integral part of this magnificent universe.

What are Your Gifts?

Loving yourself means valuing and accepting yourself for who you are. Notice what is easy and fun for you. These are your gifts! If your gifts are hard to see, it could be because they come so naturally to you that you're not used to paying attention to them.

You can ask those closest to you what they value in you, or you can often see your gifts mirrored in the people around you. For example, what do your friends, co-workers, and family often thank you for? Those are your gifts! Instead of dismissing praise and gratitude as we are so often conditioned to do, celebrate it and join in. Write down the nice things people say about you and put them where you will see them every day.

Are you a good friend? Honest? Creative? Give yourself a gold star on the calendar every time you see those qualities in yourself. Positive feedback is key to strengthening these new habits of kindness and appreciation for yourself that you are forming.

Practice: Hook-Ups

So how do we begin to relax and get comfortable with who we are? How do we lay the groundwork for the confident expression of our authentic selves? One of my favorite tools for moving out of a stressed feeling is called Hook-Ups. It's part of the Brain Gym® program developed by Paul and Gail Dennison.

I taught this technique to Myrna when she was a new doctor at the local hospital. She often felt intimidated when she had to sit at the meeting table and report to older, mostly male, doctors. She started using Hook-Ups right there at those meetings, and she was amazed at how fast it worked, "That puts me into a relaxed state faster than Transcendental Meditation!" she told me.

She would sit at the table, cross her ankles, and then cross her wrists in her lap. To everyone seated around the table, she didn't look like she was doing anything out of the ordinary. She shared that she felt much more comfortable speaking up, like she was sitting with friends who trusted and respected her instead of with intimidating superiors waiting to catch her in a mistake. She could now see that the other doctors accepted her contributions to the discussions warmly and thoughtfully, and she fell in love with her career all over again. That's what creating a life you love is all about–finding ways to show up as your whole, authentic self in every situation.

Here's how I do Hook-Ups:

1. Start by standing or sitting comfortably.
2. Cross your ankles.
3. Extend your arms out in front of you, backs of the hands facing each other.
4. Cross one wrist over the other, now your hands are palm to palm.
5. Interlace your fingers and rest your clasped hands on your lap or on your chest.
6. Rest your tongue on the roof of your mouth, just behind your front teeth.
7. Hold this position for five to six deep, even breaths.
8. Uncross your ankles and unclasp your hands.
9. Bring your fingertips together and hold them for a few seconds.

This simple exercise is powerful because it integrates the two sides of our brain and connects the right side to the left side and the front to the back of our bodies.This helps us regulate our emotions, ground us in our bodies, become more mindfully aware, and even increase the flow of energy in our bodies. In other words, it moves us out of the flight, fright, freeze response to a more resourceful state of mind.

I encourage you to try Hook-Ups whenever you're feeling stressed, scattered, overwhelmed, or disconnected from yourself–for example before taking an exam or initiating a conversation where you might feel vulnerable. Use it as a way to come home to your body, to gather all the parts of yourself that may have felt separate. Notice whether it brings a sense of calm.

I go into Hook-Ups whenever I want to stay present with uncomfortable emotions or feel more at home in my body. It has taught me that I have the power to get out of fear and self- judgment again and again.

As you practice opening to the love all around you, remember to include yourself in that circle of love. You're not separate from the world. You're an integral, valuable part of the Universe. The more you recognize and appreciate the love in your everyday interactions, the easier it becomes to see yourself as worthy of that same love.

Now that we've learned to relax in stressful situations and we can see the love that surrounds us, you might be wondering, "If love is everywhere, why is it so hard for me to care for myself?"

Why Is It So Hard for Me to Care for Myself?

Don't worry, you're not alone in asking this question. In fact, it's one of the most common hurdles I see people face on their journey to self-love. The truth is, there are often deep-rooted reasons why self-love doesn't come easily. Most of them start with traumas we don't even remember. Difficulty experiencing love can originate during birth, while we were in the womb, or it can even go back to traumas that our parents or grandparents endured.

In the next chapter, we'll look into some of the biggest obstacles to self-love and I'll share how to start clearing those old patterns that have been holding you back.

Chapter Four
The Struggle is Real (and Normal!)

When I looked back and read what I wrote at the beginning of Chapter One, an alarm went off and my whole body screamed NO!!! YOU CANNOT LOVE YOURSELF!!! I have been working toward self-love for decades, and I still have to fight old beliefs that I am not lovable and love is frightening..

I am getting better at caring for myself, speaking kindly to myself, noticing when I create beauty and refraining from judging myself when things don't go well. But why is this so hard? If we are beloved creations formed in a perfect image, why do we feel so much loathing toward ourselves? Whatever term we use for the Source, All That Is, God, Spirit, Allah, Krishna, Buddha, Nature, if we're all swimming in the same sea, why do we feel so disconnected?

It took more than a half a lifetime to piece together a lot of details that allowed me to understand some of my behaviors.

Love is connection. It is a way to connect with all of creation that many of us don't even realize we have. There's an explanation for this. When we were children, we were curious and we explored. Mother wouldn't let us put fingers in outlets. The hot soup was kept out of reach, though it smelled so good. There were so many things we couldn't and shouldn't do. When we tried to connect to the world with all of our senses, we often heard, "No!" It stuck with us. It's difficult to say "Yes!!" to something we have always understood to be off-limits.

I mentioned in Chapter One that I spent most of my life feeling like I was allergic to love, and the reason was a mystery to me for most of my life. It took more than a half a lifetime to piece together a lot of details that allowed me to understand some of my behaviors. Photographs of myself as a toddler clearly show that I was a sad little girl. Two very intuitive ladies helped me to understand why. Using their information, I asked questions and received information that helped me to piece it together.

My relationship with my mother was complex, to say the least. She was a frightened and overwhelmed 26-year-old when I was born, far from her own family support system at a time when the world was changing rapidly. Her fear and loneliness during pregnancy and childbirth affected me before I took my first breath, her chemicals of fear and anxiety entered my tiny body through my umbilical cord. Her patterns became my patterns.

My brother's birth, 16 months after my birth, was also traumatic. My mother was scared and angry because my dad hadn't kept the driveway clear of snow, and they couldn't get out to take her to the doctor. The stress chemicals that flooded my brother's newborn body caused the muscle at the bottom of his stomach to spasm shut, and stop digestion, a helpful response if you're running away from a tiger and your muscles need all your energy to keep you alive. For baby Bob, the blocked stomach caused projectile vomiting. He looked like he might die. Doctors at that time didn't know that gently rubbing his stomach could relax the muscles and before he was a week old, he had surgery.

Mom and Dad took Bob to the hospital and sent me to stay with a babysitter for about ten days.

As toddlers do, I centered myself as the cause of my removal from the family. I may have surmised, "I must not be as important as this boy." I remember a cigar with "It's a boy!" printed on the label. I learned that love could be withdrawn at any moment, so why invest myself in it? Still, I went through much of my life desperately wishing for the courage to love and to receive love.

My father's parents, especially his dad, didn't shower him with the kind of affection I yearned for because, in their world, it was impractical. He grew up at a time when families guarded their hearts against the all-too-common tragedy of losing a child, and his parents had already buried three infants by the time he was born. So it didn't occur to my father when he had children of his own that they would seek affection.

But oh, how I wanted my father's affection and approval!

We don't have to keep lugging around the emotional baggage we've inherited.

At the age of 80, he tried, awkwardly, to open his heart to me. He told me that on the farm growing up, he knew he was loved because he had a roof over his head. The only way he remembered his father expressing love was by saying, "You know, you come in handy sometimes."

Me, I needed a little more convincing.

Your Soul's Signature

The way I see it, we are each radiating our own unique frequency, like a radio signal, and we attract situations that have a similar vibration to what our soul is already carrying. The situations we attract to ourselves are sometimes difficult, but there's always a reason. As I look back at my most trying times I can see how they were followed by a greater conscious awareness and therefore growth. It appears that the difficult times provided the exact opportunity I needed for my soul to grow.

What I have found interesting is that when we take responsibility for our own lives and our thoughts, we have power. We can then change our lives and move in the direction we want to go, focusing on what we love.

We don't have to keep lugging around the emotional baggage we've inherited. We can set it down, open it up, and examine our old beliefs and fears. Once we understand where they came from, we can decide whether they still serve us or it's time to let them go. This is a big part of what self-love is about. It's about recognizing that you are not defined by the fears and limitations of past generations. You are your own person, worthy of love simply because you exist.

The Science of Early Conditioning

Research shows that our experiences can actually change how our genes work, meaning that stress and trauma can be passed down through generations. Imagine that! The anxiety and fears of our parents and even grandparents live on in our cells.

During my mother's pregnancy and at my birth, I experienced a disastrous cocktail of fear and physical pain. I came into this world at a birthing home in Daggett, Michigan. I did not feel that my life was celebrated when I was born. In fact, it felt like hell.

During that time there was a common practice in childbirth called "twilight sleep". where women were given a combination of morphine for pain relief and scopolamine, which caused amnesia. The idea was to allow women to give birth without consciously experiencing or remembering the pain of labor. However, the reality of twilight sleep was far more disturbing than many realized at the time.

Women under twilight sleep weren't unconscious. Many thrashed violently, raged, and behaved erratically, almost as if possessed. They were aware during the birth, but the drugs prevented them from forming memories of the experience. Can you imagine the trauma this could cause, both for the mother and the newborn?

Research shows that our experiences can actually change how our genes work.

Now, you might be wondering, what does this have to do with self-love and early conditioning? Well, think about it. A newborn comes into the world, and instead of being greeted by an alert, present mother, they're met with someone behaving in ways that could be terrifying for a tiny, sensitive being. The mother, upon waking, has no memory of the birth experience or how she behaved. This severe disruption to the bonding process could have profound effects on both mother and child.

In my case, I'm not sure if my mother was given twilight sleep, but I do know she was terrified and unprepared for childbirth. She didn't have her mother and sisters to help her, since they had recently moved away. My mother was rumored to have asked the doctor, "How is the baby going to get out?"

I can picture it. My mother in a nightmarish state of anguish, her spasming muscles refusing to relax. The doctor resorted to breaking my collar bone to squeeze my shoulders through the birth canal. He twisted my small body as he pulled, also breaking the lowest vertebra.

My mother couldn't breastfeed me, probably because I cried from the pain of my fractured collar bone when she held me, so I got by on cow's milk.

These cultural messages and the effects of our early experiences seep into our psyche, often without us even realizing it.

Going back further, there was shame and loneliness. World War II had just ended when my mother was pregnant with me. Returning soldiers competed for the jobs women held, and she may have worn a girdle to hide her growing belly. Facing her first pregnancy without the support of her family, she must have felt overwhelmed and alone.

Neuroscience tells us that our infant brains are like sponges, soaking up everything around us. The experiences we have in the womb, as babies and young children literally shape the structure of our brains, forming pathways that can last a lifetime. That's why those early feelings of being unwanted, alone in the world, an extra burden, or a source of pain can stick with us for so long.

These early experiences set the stage for how we see ourselves and the world around us. They form the foundation of our beliefs about whether we're lovable, whether we're worthy, whether we're enough.

Cultural Conditioning Shapes Us Too

It's not just our family histories and early childhood experiences that tell us who we are. The culture we grow up in plays a huge role too. For many of us who grew up in the mid-20th century, there were clear expectations about how boys and girls should behave, what they were capable of, and what their value was.

I remember looking into my brother's crib and realizing he had something I didn't have. He was a boy! I thought, "That must be why I'm not important." I only knew two things about my little brothers: they were boys, and they were very special.

Would I have been that special if I had been born a boy? I wanted my parents' love desperately, but if that was what it took to win my parents' love, I didn't have a chance.

These cultural messages and the effects of our early experiences seep into our psyche, often without us even realizing it. They become part of the story we tell ourselves about who we are and what we're worth. They're like scripts that we follow, shaping how we see the world and ourselves in ways we often don't even realize.

(the exercise we did back in Chapter One) is an excellent way to establish a new, kinder way of thinking about ourselves. Here are some positive statements to use while tapping:

- I ground myself into the present moment.
- I inhale peace and exhale stress.
- I know things can and do work out for me.
- I see the events of my day unfolding efficiently with harmony–and they do!
- The universe rushes in to support what I am committed to do and I am thankful.
- I journal my desired outcomes, and the Universe (God) clearly knows my intentions because I write them down.
- I envision win-win outcomes for all of my activities.
- I act on the wisdom of my "still small voice."

Breaking the Cycle

I know things have gotten pretty heavy in this chapter, but we are coming up on the silver lining. While early conditioning may put a damper on our self-worth and ability to love ourselves, it's not the whole story. Our brains remain flexible throughout our lives, meaning we can change our deeply held beliefs about ourselves. Once we become aware of the things we have been conditioned to believe about ourselves, we can, with compassionate understanding, begin to change them. The events behind these condition beliefs are often the source of buried treasure—golden nuggets of motivation, inspiration and compassion for others.

Excavating these treasures isn't always easy though, and it certainly isn't accomplished overnight. It involves asking ourselves, "what have I learned as a result of living through this difficult situation?"Whenever negative thoughts and feelings come up, as they will according to long-established habits, we can choose to focus on what we have learned, the truths we've discovered.

This type of learning involves more than taking information into your brain. We need to know what we know in our hearts and bodies as well as our minds. This requires lots of practice and conscious choice. We need to choose self-love over and over, until it becomes a habit. Until it becomes as natural as taking that next breath.

The goal is not to try to become numb to your past or to erase it or pretend nothing bad ever happened. Instead, we're working to understand where our beliefs come from, recognize when they're no longer serving us, and consciously choose new, more loving ways of relating to ourselves.

Getting Out of Ruts and Blazing New Trails

A big part of cultivating self-love is replacing old habitual thoughts and attitudes about ourselves with new, compassionate and appreciative ways of seeing ourselves.

Our habitual thought patterns are like ruts in an old dirt road. Just like a Model T's narrow wheels would get stuck following the same tracks over and over, our thoughts tend to travel along well-worn neural pathways in our brains. These deep ruts of negative self-talk can feel impossible to escape. They can really limit what we feel capable of achieving.

But you know what? We're not driving Model Ts anymore. We know so much more about our brains and how they're wired, it's like we've upgraded from that spindly Model T to a modern off-road vehicle with wide, grippy tires. We have tools and techniques at our disposal that our parents and grandparents couldn't even imagine.

Forgiveness starts with understanding.

We now understand that our brains can form new neural connections throughout life. We have access to techniques that can literally rewire our brains and create positive thought patterns that bypass those old, rutted roads entirely.

Practice: Butterfly Hug

When your mind starts racing, your muscles tense up, your breath is shallow--that's stress! The first thing to do is to calm your nervous system. The Butterfly Hug is great for that. Here's how to do it.

Cross your arms over your chest and tap each upper arm, first one arm and then the other, while breathing slowly. Switching back and forth between left and right helps calm your body and brings your mind back into a more peaceful state. Give yourself a Butterfly Hug any time you want to relax your body and calm your mind.

Once you experience how fast you can move out of a stress response, it will be easy to put this special skill into practice when needed. Forming new brain habits takes time, but it's worth the effort! The beauty of modern, neuroscience-based approaches like this is that they work with your brain's natural tendencies, not against them. It's like having a GPS that can reroute you around those old ruts, guiding you onto more kind, positive paths of thinking and responding.

Even with tools like this at our disposal, developing self-love is going to take work. This is especially true if you've spent years or decades believing you're not worthy of it. But I promise you, it's worth the effort. The joy, peace, and fulfillment that come from truly loving yourself are beyond measure. The best part is that this love is always available to you. It's not dependent on anyone else or any external circumstance.

The Power of Forgiveness

With all this talk about how deeply our early experiences can affect us, you might be feeling a bit overwhelmed. Maybe you're thinking about your own childhood, your parents, or the cultural messages you internalized, and old feelings of anger or resentment have been triggered. That happens! Sometimes stirring up these old memories can feel like too much. You could call a good friend, talk to a spiritual adviser or set up an appointment with a counselor. Talking or journaling is extremely helpful for moving the energy so that it leaves your body.

Forgiveness is one of the most powerful tools I've found for breaking free from destructive thoughts and behaviors that, although they may be directed at others, hurt one person way more than anyone else—you.

Forgiveness isn't about condoning harm or pretending everything is okay. It's about freeing yourself from the burden of resentment and pain. When we become aware of what we don't like, forgive it, and focus on what we **do** like, we free our life force and can raise our vibration and improve our health.

A lack of forgiveness doesn't necessarily mean that you're going around feeling angry or holding a grudge against someone. Most of the day-to-day forgiveness we're called to do is related to judging ourselves and others, whether unconsciously or consciously. When we have critical thoughts, even though we may keep it to ourselves and never express what we're thinking, negative thoughts still get in the way of our ability to love ourselves.

One simple example of being critical was when I noticed that somebody I was in a class with needed a haircut. What other people do with their hair isn't usually a concern of mine, but this time I noticed it. I forgot about it until I went home and looked in the mirror. It was then I realized that **I** was the one who was due for a trim. Once I'd been to my hairdresser, I felt a lot better!

When we make changes in ourselves, our view of the outside world magically changes.

Forgiveness can release a torrent of emotions that we may not even know we're carrying. Let me tell you a story about forgiveness that unfolds in layers of realization and awareness.

When I was sent to stay with a babysitter at age two and a half, the babysitter's father sexually molested me. I had no conscious memory of that. It was deeply buried with emotions that were too frightening for a toddler. The search to understand myself took half a century and I was elated when the pieces were uncovered.

I learned of the abuse with the help of two psychics, one who pinpointed the age at which I was deeply wounded, and the other who retrieved the name, "Carl." When I asked my parents who Carl was, they told me, beaming, that he was my babysitter's father. That early experience at the babysitters taught me two things—first, how to create pleasure in my body, and second, that feelings of bodily pleasure were frightening and shameful. The experience also reinforced the habit I had from birth of leaving my body to avoid discomfort.

I didn't realize how angry I was until, through serendipitous events, I felt anger in my body and released it. When my partner pulled up on my arm to make me raise my lower leg in a Latin dance class, I was surprised to feel anger flooding my body. The magnitude of the emotions erupting were far out of proportion to the indignation I felt in the moment. At the time, I didn't know about the sexual abuse when I was a toddler or the injuries at birth. I couldn't imagine where all that intense anger was coming from.

Establishing a strong habit of self-forgiveness is a big part of creating a life we can love.

Around the same time I attended a breathwork seminar. While we were lying on our backs, kicking our feet like children in a tantrum, the facilitator came by and told me to say, "fuck you," so I did, and again, a torrent of anger was unleashed. I still had no idea where the emotions came from.

Forgiveness starts with understanding. I started forgiving my dad for being so emotionally distant when he showed me the graves of the three infants his parents had buried on the farm. I saw that he had learned at a young age how parents could be hurt by bonding with children at a time when infant death was common.

Realizing how isolated my mother felt helped me to forgive her too. She complained to me about my father as if I were a friend or sister, not an adolescent girl. I resented that because I wanted to keep my dad on a pedestal.

When I learned of my birth trauma and the sexual abuse I had experienced when I was very young, I understood that my parents truly did love me, and they were doing the best with the knowledge and resources they had at the time.

We can extend this understanding to the societies we live in. The gender expectations that made me feel less valuable as a girl weren't created to hurt me personally. They were misguided attempts to make sense of the power that the masculine holds in our culture.

Forgiving doesn't mean forgetting or excusing. It means acknowledging what happened, feeling the pain of it, and then consciously choosing to release the hold it has on you. It's saying, "This happened, and it hurt me. But I'm not going to let it control my life anymore."

Thus, when we forgive, we create space for new patterns to emerge. We free up the energy that was tied up in resentment and direct it toward loving ourselves and creating the life we want.

Here is a practice to help you feel the power of forgiveness all through your being—in your heart, your mind, and every cell of your body.

Four Simple Phrases for Self-Forgiveness

When I first learned about Ho'oponopono, the Hawaiian practice of forgiveness and reconciliation, I was struck by its beautiful simplicity. Four short phrases that I could hardly believe created such profound change:

"I'm sorry. Please forgive me. Thank you. I love you."

I was searching to understand why my mind seemed to function so differently from others when I came across the story of a psychologist who used a traditional Hawaiian method to heal an entire ward of dangerous psychiatric patients who had committed horrifying violent crimes (Vitale and Len, 2009). He succeeded in bringing them peace and healing—without ever seeing them in person! He simply sat with their files and worked as a shaman does in the spiritual realm. He had learned from traditional Hawaiian Huna teachers.

In his heart, he took full responsibility for the condition of the inmates as a part of our shared consciousness. In other words, he sincerely practiced becoming his brother's keeper.

I decided to use the short form to see whether I could forgive myself and release myself from daily stubborn self-judgments. I did begin to see myself with greater compassion. My story isn't as dramatic as that of the psychiatric patients, but I found that a doorway opened to more ease, freedom, and compassion in my life. It has been a quick way to shift negative self-talk.

Here's how to practice a simple form of Ho'oponopono:

1. Ground yourself and take several slow, deep breaths.
2. Place your attention in your heart center.
3. Bring to mind the situation or relationship needing forgiveness.
4. From your heart, repeat these phrases:

"I'm sorry"
"Please forgive me"
"Thank you"
"I love you."

What makes this practice so powerful is that it works at the deep level at which we are all connected. When we see something that disturbs us in another person, it's usually a reflection of something within ourselves that needs healing, just like in my haircut story.

By taking complete responsibility for our experience and choosing love over judgment, we create space for profound change within—and the changes we make to our inner lives are guaranteed to be reflected in our outer experiences.

While honoring the Hawaiian roots of this practice, I encourage you to make it personally meaningful. Some find it helpful to write the phrases with pen and paper, speak them out loud, or trace them in the air with a finger.

You can use them in the moment when you are triggered, and you can make a habit of saying them when you wake up each morning so that you will be slower to judge yourself or others when triggered throughout the day.

You can even apply the four statements to past situations as part of healing from old wounds.

However you practice, the key is to say the four phrases of Ho'oponopono with your whole heart while taking responsibility for the way you experience your own life. Although most people who know about the practice associate it with that Hawaiian psychiatric hospital, this practice is potent as a method of self-care. Every time you forgive yourself instead of passing judgment, you are healing not just your own self, you are contributing to the healing of the collective consciousness.

It has taken me a long time to realize that I need to and can use this forgiveness technique on myself. Whenever I notice that I am sabotaging myself, I can recognize it, forgive it and let the old belief go in the moment. I didn't realize how often I judged and mentally berated myself until I started this practice. I haven't completely kicked the habit yet, but catching myself and forgiving myself each time it happens has already made a huge difference in terms of the ease with which I live my life.

Establishing a strong habit of self-forgiveness is a big part of creating a life we can love.

Bookmark this page. Forgiveness is a process, not a one-time event. It's something you will need to do over and over again. Each time you choose forgiveness, you break free from old patterns and open the door to greater self-compassion.

Understand that this will take time and effort. If you've been trying to take better care of yourself and cultivate positive habits in your life for a long time, and nothing seems to stick, I want you to know that you're not alone. You may have tried all the self-help techniques, positive affirmations, New Year's resolutions, you name it, only to find yourself falling back into old patterns.

Don't give up. You can place visual cues in your home to remind you to take small steps toward creating a life you love, like putting stars on the calendar when you forgive yourself. I like writing kind notes to myself on my bathroom mirror.

The path to self-love isn't a straight line. Some days you might feel like you're making great progress, and other days you might feel like you're right back where you started.

Loving yourself enough to treat yourself well takes serious, sustained effort. It's not something that happens overnight, and it's certainly not something you can force through sheer willpower alone. So don't feel bad if you haven't mastered it yet.

It is indeed hard to do. But it is do-able. Remember that underwater painting I saw at the art fair? The one that made me smile for the first time in what felt like forever? Well, remember that it took me years to finally allow myself to buy a similar painting for myself. Years! That's how ingrained our patterns of self-denial can be.

The path to self-love isn't a straight line. It's more like a winding road with plenty of bumps, potholes, and unexpected turns. Some days you might feel like you're making great progress, and other days you might feel like you're right back where you started. That's okay. As a certain little cartoon fish said, "Just keep swimming."

What matters more than anything is that you keep showing up for yourself, day after day. Each time you choose a loving thought over a critical one, each time you do something kind for yourself, you're making it easier to continue speaking encouragingly to yourself.

It takes practice, like learning to play an instrument or speak a new language. So be patient with yourself. Celebrate each small victory. And most importantly, keep going. You're not failing if you haven't mastered self-love yet—you're learning. And that learning process is beautiful and valuable in itself.

Chapter Five
Come Home to Your Body

I mentioned in Chapter Four that two of my bones were broken when I was born, my collarbone and the lowest vertebra. Birth is the time when soul and body are meant to come together. But when I was being born, I suspect that I didn't want to go into that broken, vulnerable, hurting little body. It was too painful! I believe this is why I've always been more comfortable in the realms of spirit than the physical. I don't know how many times friends have had to say to me, "Earth to Linda," in an attempt to get my full attention. Spirit is our first home, and for me it's the home I ran to in order to avoid the pain in my new body. Maybe because of that early experience or because of who I Am, spirit is where I'm most comfortable.

When you look at your body as a gift on loan, it becomes that much more precious.

Pain isn't the only obstacle I have worked with to fully inhabit my body. It has taken me a long time to learn to allow myself to experience physical pleasure too.

I have certain gifts associated with the ability to leave my body when I am stressed. I have a strong sixth sense and can usually intuit what's going on with people—where they're experiencing pain or discomfort. So I was taken by surprise when a colleague told me that my work would be even more healing if I climbed into my body and worked from that vantage point.

What did she mean by that? My interest was piqued because I wanted to do whatever I could to become a better healer. I was also puzzled because I thought I already lived in my body. I knew well enough when I was hungry, tired, cold, and needed to use the bathroom...but apparently, there was more to it than that. I had—and still have—so much to learn!

Even now, after being on this quest for four decades, or more, I'm still finding out how important it is to ground myself in my body, and sometimes I feel like I'm starting to get the hang of it.

I have to remember to call myself into my body, every day, in every moment. Becoming present and staying present for me is a conscious act of self-care that I choose over and over again and reinforce through grounding practices. Often, when I get into my car, I consciously bring my awareness behind my eyes.

I don't practice perfectly. Sometimes, even though I know it would be better to ground myself, in a moment of perceived danger, physical or emotional, I still flee.

From Connection to Disconnection and Back Again

You may have heard people say that there's more to life than what we experience in our physical bodies, that we are spiritual beings having a physical experience and not the other way around. This rang true for me when I first heard it. What I've had to learn in this lifetime is to ground my spiritual self into my body and consciously listen to and follow the guidance of my intuition, that still small voice.

I've had to learn to value the care and feeding of the body I live in, and know that it is something to cherish, temporary as it is. When you look at your body as a gift on loan, something you only get to spend a short amount of time in, it becomes that much more precious. Even if you didn't have a traumatic birth like mine, life has a way of slowly weakening the original connection to our authentic selves and what we love, often turning our focus to pleasing others. It happens in little ways, day by day, especially when we're young.

Every experience we had as young children taught us something about who we were and how to get along in the world. We learned how to fit in, how to be "good," how to keep the peace. That often meant ignoring what our bodies were telling us. Maybe you felt scared, but everyone said there was nothing to be afraid of. Or you were angry, but were told, "Nice girls don't get mad." Or your belly was full, but were made to clean your plate anyway.

Little by little, we learned to distrust our own physical experiences and our intuitive "knowings." We started to believe that the people around us know better than our own bodies, hearts, and minds.

Each time we experience stress, it's important to reconnect through breathing and grounding practices.

As adults, however, there are times when we are able to make a conscious choice instead of following our early programming. We can do this by calming our minds, grounding ourselves in our bodies, dropping into our hearts, and listening with kindness. Then we can respond instead of automatically reacting to what's going on around us and within us. Make enough of these conscious choices, and they start to become a habit!

Everyday stresses also disconnect us from our bodies. We modern humans tend to spend more time than is good for us in a state of stress. We're on high alert, our bodies prepared to fight off threats or run from danger. When we're poised to react, muscles tense and breath shallow, it's virtually impossible to go into a flow state and live a life filled with synchronistic miracles and the joy that they bring. As a result, we lose touch with that deep inner knowing that comes from being fully present in our bodies.

This is why, each time we experience stress, it's important to reconnect through breathing and grounding practices.

For me, grounding in my body as my own personal home-base on this planet has been one of the hardest parts of self-love. We're never truly disconnected from our bodies, but if we don't feel that connection and fully embrace it, it's not going to do us much good.

Grounding is Self-Care

Love is all about connection, right? Self-love means loving all aspects of who we are—bodies, egos and all. Our bodies are more than just vehicles for our minds and spirits. When we treat them as somehow separate from our "true" selves, we are rejecting a fundamental part of our being. Here is an example where pain and expense could have been prevented by being grounded into my body:

In August of 2023, I was driving on a narrow winding road in the mountains of North Carolina. It was dark and raining when headlights appeared. Pulling over to make room, I felt my right front tire lurching downward toward the roaring creek barreling downhill, as the force of the water seemed to pull my car closer to danger. Horrified, I put on the brakes.

V-e-r-r-r-y s l-o-o-w-l y, I pushed the heavy door of my leaning car open–which was tilted precariously at a 30-degree angle toward the creek.

I tried to call AAA. No signal. Tense with fear, I slid out of the car. I was terrified that looking into the creek, four feet below, would cause my van to fall to its ruin. I had learned that when I focus on what I don't want, it is more likely to occur because I'm giving it more energy. I was not about to add any thought energy that might push the van over the edge.

Our beliefs are creating our experiences all the time.

When I started walking, I found that moving my body helped dissipate the energy of fear. Speaking out loud, I asked my guardian angels to protect my car.

In my friend's home the next day, I was still in shock and hadn't fully returned to my body. That's when I tripped and grabbed for what I thought was a big, solid recliner. Crap! It was actually a swiveling rocking chair! I would have been better off dropping to the floor. Instead, the muscles inside of my thigh broke my leg as I did the sideway splits.

That experience really drove home for me how important it is to be present in my body. When we're not grounded, when we're not fully here, we can hurt ourselves! We miss the signals our bodies are sending us, the instincts that could keep us safe.

Grounding Gives Us Superpowers

Being in our bodies helps us tune into the knowledge that is available in our hearts. Being grounded brings us into the present moment. We are not worrying about the future, trying to plan how things should be, or mulling over past events. We are in the now, able to experience gratefully each moment, whatever that experience is. When I say that grounding gives us superpowers, I don't mean that it gives us the ability to fly around zapping bad guys. The present is where we have power, the power to make changes. We can make adjustments to steer our lives in the way we want them to go when we are present. We can keep ourselves safer and make better choices. And staying present supports us in doing the best that we can by becoming aware of unconscious beliefs about ourselves that may be "running the show behind the scenes."

Becoming aware of negative unconscious beliefs allows us to install more positive beliefs out of which our lives are created, just as we were talking about in the last chapter. Every day we are making hundreds of choices. Being present in our bodies helps us remember what we value. Then we can make clear, conscious choices about whether to have a sugary snack or some healthy nuts and seeds that we keep handy. It's these small choices that determine the quality of our lives.

Our beliefs, whether they are conscious thoughts or repetitive ideas running the show from behind the scenes, are creating our experiences all the time. It's a big "aha" moment when you realize this. **Everything in your life—the good and the challenging—has been shaped by your thoughts, perceptions, and unconscious beliefs.** When you're grounded in your body and know what's important to you, you can't help but become aware of this process. You can then start to direct it consciously.

Grounding allows your energy, which is one and the same with the energy of the cosmos, to move through and around you. When we're grounded, this energy flows smoothly, connecting us to the Earth below and the cosmos above.

Intuition and all the other spiritual gifts are not just in our heads. They're whole-body experiences.

With practice, we can learn to tap into this flow, and magical things start to happen. We might find that things we need just seem to appear. People who can help us show up at just the right time. We become co-creators with God, or the universe, or whatever you want to call that greater force. We don't have to settle for being passive observers of our lives. We're active participants, using our amazing bodies as the instruments through which we create our reality.

Here is an excellent example of what can happen when you're in the flow. When my friend invited me to a Zoom introduction to the authors of a collaborative book she was part of, I heard Laura Fox speak about how she helps people write books sharing what they had learned. Instantly, I knew that Laura was the person who could help me get through my creative impasse. I felt great gratitude for my need being supplied. I knew immediately that with her help, I could actually finish in spite of limited writing experience and a habit of leaving my body when stressed.

I know personally that it's not easy to hang out in our bodies. When we do, we feel absolutely everything—the good and the bad. That can be pretty uncomfortable. The temptation to disconnect and float above it all is real. But when we do that, we miss out on some of the most joyful experiences life throws our way.

I remember as a kid, riding my bicycle, feeling the breeze flowing through my hair. I was 12 years old. A song came through me that flowed as naturally as my breath, even though the words didn't mean much to me at the time.

Fear and pain and guilt and shame

Oh, let me get out of this pain!
I've no more need of this suffering and greed
Oh, let me get out of this pain!

Forgive! Forgive!
My dear loving Angel, I forgive you.

Those words felt like they came out of nowhere at the time, but as I grew the song became a guiding anthem. It showed me that the way through the pain I carried was to forgive and cherish my higher self as my own dear, loving Angel.

How did a 12-year-old access such profound wisdom? By riding my bike and opening my mouth to let flow whatever words wanted to come.

Dancing is another great way to bring the spiritual into the physical, and there's sound science behind why activities like bike riding and dancing can unlock our intuition and creativity. There's a reason we spiritual beings choose to have bodies! When our bodies and spirits work together, we can create truly amazing things.

When we're fully in our bodies, present in the moment, our brain shifts gears. It's like we're turning down the volume on that chattering, critical voice in our heads and tuning into a different channel. Suddenly, we can hear the whispers of our intuition, the sparks of creativity that are always there, just waiting for us to notice.

If you think about it for a minute, you can probably come up with an example from your own life, like my bike riding experience. How many times have you had a brilliant idea pop into your head while you were in the shower, taking a walk, or doing something else physical? That's not a coincidence. It's your brain and body working together, creating the perfect conditions for inspiration to strike.

Intuition and all the other spiritual gifts are not just in our heads. They're whole-body experiences. That's why so many psychics and healers start their work by grounding themselves. They're doing more than just clearing their minds!

Just Breathe

To allow the healing power of love in, we need to fully inhabit our bodies and feel our connection to the Earth. This creates a stable foundation for the work that we're here to do. Then, from that grounded place, we can reach out and connect with higher energies more effectively.

Rebuilding your connection to your body starts with the most simple, basic thing we know how to do, and that is to breathe. When we inhale deeply and exhale slowly, we're sending a message to our bodies: "I'm safe now. The danger has passed." Go ahead and tell that scared, disconnected child inside, "It's okay to come home to your body now."

Breathe in, breathe out.

With each breath, each moment of awareness, you are chipping away at that wall between your body/mind and your spirit. Simply focus on your breathing, feeling it coming through your nostrils, the cooling air in your sinuses. Feel your abdomen and chest expand and then contract repeatedly. Allow it to gradually become easier to trust what your body naturally does. Allow yourself to open up to a whole world of wisdom that's been there all along, just waiting for you to listen.

Birth Healing Meditation

Many of us carry wounds from before or during birth that have made it challenging to fully inhabit our bodies. This meditation may help to heal those wounds and honor our physical existence.

Find a quiet space where you won't be disturbed. Close your eyes and take several deep breaths, allowing yourself to relax.

Visualize your parents as they were around the time you were conceived. See them sitting together, perhaps having their morning coffee. Observe their youthful faces, their hopes, and their fears as it sinks in that they are about to become parents.

Now, imagine standing before them as your current self. Take this opportunity let them know how you feel about the body they gave you. Speak to them out loud or in your mind. You can also do this as a journal exercise.

Some people begin with, "Mom and Dad, thank you for..."

As you speak or write from your heart, you might envision any worries or concerns your parents might have had dissolving from their faces and their posture. If there were fears about the future, your presence before them is proof that they were successful, they got you through the tough times to adulthood.

Becoming aware of negative unconscious beliefs allows us to install more positive beliefs.

Now, do your parents have anything to say to you? What do

you hear? What do you feel? Write down any impressions, no matter how subtle.

This practice can bring peace to the anxieties that might have surrounded your conception and early existence. It acknowledges the sacred connection between you and your parents, honoring your origins and the gift of your physical form.

Remember, you chose this body, this life, for profound reasons. By reconnecting with your earliest moments in this physical form, you reaffirm your decision to be here, in this body, at this time.

After the meditation, journal about your experience. What emotions arose? What insights did you gain? How do you feel about your body and your existence now?

Any Movement Will Do

Remember the Tapping and Hook-Ups you learned in Chapters One and Three? If you skipped over them, go back and try them out now! They are also great for helping you ground in your body. Any kind of physical activity is, actualy—dancing, vocalizing, riding a bicycle, doing yoga. If you're feeling unsure about it or uncomfortable, you can always start small by lifting one shoulder or tapping first one foot and then the other.

Bring the Light into Your Body

Any time you feel that your body is weighed down by heavy energies, you can fill it with light by doing this exercise:

Imagine you are a tree with a taproot going down from the bottoms of your feet all the way to the center of the Earth. Then, from the top of your head, send a white beam into the cosmos, all the way to your soul star above your head. From that point, imagine powerful pure white light flowing into your body. This light is so intense that your natural eyes would have to look away. The light fills your body, flowing into every one of your 30 trillion cells, cleansing and revitalizing them. Then the brilliant light moves out from your body into your energy field, transmuting whatever is less than the pure light of Source that you are.

Chapter Six
Body Wisdom

Remember in the last chapter when I told you about my colleague who suggested I "climb into my body" to be more present to my chiropractic clients? Learning to inhabit my body, it turned out, taught me a lot more than how to be a better healer. I thought I already knew the human body inside out, but as I began to explore my own body, asking it questions and listening to what it had to say, I discovered a whole new world of wisdom that had been there all along, just waiting for me to tune in.

As you start to get more familiar with your body, keep in mind it's simply giving you information that you can use to feel better.

Your body is pretty amazing, when you think about it. Yes, it's the vehicle that allows your spirit to create, move around in and experience this physical world to the maximum. But that's not the only benefit to living in a human body.

Your Body Is Your Friend

I would like to introduce you to your body as an ally with intelligence all its own. It has so much to tell you about how to heal, how to protect yourself, and how to experience life to the fullest. Learning to listen to these messages takes practice, and yes, it's something we all need to work at. But it's a skill set anyone can develop.

Whenever I practice tuning-in to my body, I pick up on certain cues. Holding my breath or a tightness in my shoulders when I'm stressed, a twinge in my lower back when I'm pushing myself too hard. A feeling of heaviness when I'm saying "yes" to something that doesn't align with my values. These are the body's way of communicating important information about our emotional and physical state. Learning to listen to these messages has shown me the way to take better care of myself by making decisions that align with the happiness and love that my soul yearns for.

Tuning into your body's wisdom isn't going to be a snap. This is especially true if, like me, you've spent years ignoring its messages. That's why in this chapter, we're going to explore various techniques to help you reconnect with your body's innate wisdom. We'll talk about how to understand the connection between your body and your mind, recognize your body's signals, and use your emotions as a compass to guide you toward what's best for you.

Your true self is your greatest strength.

As you start to get more familiar with your body and the way it speaks to you, keep in mind that the idea is not to control or conquer the body. It's not trying to be the boss of you or make you feel guilty. It's simply giving you information that you can use to feel better.

It is pretty common to feel guilty when we first start to realize how we've ignored such a great friend for so long. We push through the headaches, gulp down another energy drink to fight the fatigue, and tell ourselves we'll get enough rest "someday." Men do this because they've been told that giving into the body's needs is a sign of weakness. We women ignore our bodies because we're conditioned to think that everyone else's needs are more important than our own.

But when you listen to your body, you're tapping into a source of knowledge that goes way deeper than any diet book or wellness trend. You're connecting with your own personal guide to health, harmony and happiness. This is a guide that knows you better than anyone else possibly could.

Understanding the Mind - Body Connection

Most people go to counselors, psychologists or psychiatrists when they have troubled thoughts and emotions. They go to specialists for various organs and body parts when they have physical problems. I am an advocate of holistic health, which means taking care of the body, mind, and spirit all at once, but my approach isn't one you'll hear about much in a mainstream doctor's or therapist's office.

It is a scientifically established fact, though, that what happens in our bodies impacts our minds, and vice versa. Think about the last time you were stressed. Maybe your shoulders crept up toward your ears, or your stomach felt like it was doing somersaults. That's your mind-body connection in action! Our bodies react to our thoughts and emotions, sometimes before we even realize what we're feeling.

When you start paying attention to how your body reacts to different situations, you get clues about what's really going on in your mind and heart.

For example, do you get a headache every time you have to deal with a certain person at work? That might be your body responding to an unspoken conflict that needs to be addressed. Or maybe you notice your energy levels plummet after eating certain foods. That's valuable information about what your body needs to feel its best.

While these sensations are often uncomfortable and even painful, know that this doesn't mean your body is trying to punish you. Feeling crappy is simply a natural consequence when things are out of alignment, such as when you have a heavy-duty emotion that is inappropriate to express at the time and you suppress it. That can be the start of an energy block in your body leading to a functional difficulty and health issue. There is no intention or judgment behind it, and it certainly is not an indication of what you deserve.

I remember a time when I was walking out of the grocery store, and suddenly I felt a sharp pain in my ear. Knowing that the bones around the ears affect the nerves in the ears, I immediately put my middle fingers on my ear, my thumbs on the bone below my ears and took a deep breath moving my chin up and down with the exhale. That's how those bones move when we breathe. After doing that a few times the pain subsided. I was relieved but curious about what had happened.

After putting my groceries in my car, I sat behind the wheel, asking myself, "What happened right before the pain?" I mentally retraced the steps I had taken before walking out the door. I was at the cashier's, checking out, and pushed my cart toward the door. But then I recalled a poster that I had stared at for several minutes before leaving. It showed a working-class man smiling broadly at a kind nurse who had her hand on his shoulder. It was obviously an example of a moment of shared connection. It was a poster to let customers know that the store was providing vaccines.

In my twenties, I got a flu shot that made my fingers tingle. Even though that experience didn't immediately come to mind when I saw the poster, my body remembered. I realized then that the pain in my ears was my body's way of telling me that something I was uncomfortable with was going on.

These kinds of messages can go both ways. Just like uncomfortable thoughts can make you physically tense up, taking deep breaths and relaxing your body can help calm your mind.

To quickly release tension, cross your arms and alternately tap your right and left upper arms.

Notice the shift in your thoughts?

I stopped to do this technique while writing this and found myself spontaneously saying, "I love you, I love you, I love you," and then, "You can do this, you can do this, you can do it."

When we learn to process our emotions in a healthy way, instead of pushing them down, we free up so much energy.

Whenever you feel emotions like sadness, anger, and joy, notice where they show up in your body. Does your stomach complain? Does your chest feel light or heavy? Do any muscles tense up?

When you feel a sudden pang or twinge or cramp, ask yourself what the message could be. Check in with your emotions and your inner knowing. Recognize these "Alert!" signals for what they are, a nudge to pay attention to your thoughts or what you have taken into your mouth or maybe not released from the other end.

Sometimes the relationships between our physical sensations and thoughts are quite literal. A woman I know was about to go in for a colostomy when she had an AHA! that prevented it, simply by paying attention to her thoughts. When her supervisor walked by her desk, she noticed that she was thinking, "You give me a pain in the arse." At that moment she knew that all she needed to do to heal her colon was to quit her job. The doctors called it a miracle!

If you're not sure which thoughts are related to your aches and pains, try drinking half a glass of water just before lying down to sleep at night. Tell yourself, "When I drink the rest of this water in the morning, I will understand the cause of this feeling."

Louise Hay's *You Can Heal Your Life* has been an invaluable resource for me and my clients. My copy is dog-eared and full of highlights. Inside, she provides a comprehensive list of ailments that could be more than just physical. They could be rooted in your emotional or spiritual needs.

You might read, for example, that your headaches could be related to self-criticism, or that your lower back pain has to do with financial worries. The interpretations you find in *You Can Heal Your Life* are excellent and usually highly accurate, but they are not specific to you. Once you know what the general issue is, you can continue to dig deeper. You can ask your body questions inspired by your physical symptoms such as, which part of my financial picture is out of alignment? In what ways can I be kinder to myself?

Recognizing Your Body's Signals

Listening to your body is the best way to understand how to reduce stress and become healthier all around. Fortunately, it doesn't take hours of meditation to begin to tune in. The techniques are simple, and I'll be sharing a lot of them in the remainder of this chapter so you can pick and choose the ones that are useful to you.

It starts with simply paying attention. Some of the messages you hear are obvious, and you're likely already listening to them. Like that rumble in your tummy telling you it's lunchtime. But other messages can be a bit more subtle.

Messages about our physical needs are the easiest to recognize, so that's where we'll start. These include things like a gnawing sensation in your stomach when you're hungry, a dry mouth when you need water, or that heavy feeling in your eyelids when you're fighting off sleep.

Sometimes subtle physical sensations can clue us into emotions that we don't consciously want to deal with. Have you ever noticed how stress can make your stomach churn? Or how tight your chest gets when you're feeling anxious?

Our bodies carry emotions until we're ready to process and release them—even if this takes decades.

You might notice a slump in energy or difficulty waking up in the morning after eating certain foods, or a surge of vitality after spending time in nature. These energy shifts can tell you a lot about what nourishes you and what depletes you.

When you become fluent in the languages that your body speaks, you can begin to respond to these signals before they turn into blaring alarms.

I've found this technique that John Mullen, the creator of Palmajestics™ developed to relieve headaches helpful.

1. Place one hand on your forehead, just above your eyes.
2. Place your other hand on the back of your head, at the base of your skull.
3. Gently hold this position for 1-2 minutes, breathing deeply.
4. Notice any shifts in your thinking or emotional state.

You may notice relief from any body aches as well.

Variations on this technique have worked for me on all kinds of aches. Any time you feel sore or achy in your body try simply placing your right hand on the painful area and your left hand on the center of your chest. Hold for a couple of minutes, breathing in deeply and exhaling slowly.

Emotional Awareness Journal

At the end of each day, take a few minutes to reflect.

Ask yourself: **What emotions did I feel today?**

For each emotion, notice where you felt it in your body.

Write down what you observe, and be specific. Instead of just "I felt sad," include how your body felt at the time, for example, "I felt a heaviness in my chest when I was sad." Imagine the heaviness in your chest and ask it, "What does it want to tell you?" Note any response in your journal.

Be aware of and grateful for your emotions. They're all valid and they all provide important information.

Do this for a week and see what patterns you notice. You might be surprised at what you learn about yourself!

When we learn to process our emotions in a healthy way, instead of pushing them down, we free up so much energy. This energy is one of the ingredients we're going to need if we want to release joy in our lives.

Breaking the Stress Cycle

Stress is an unavoidable part of our days. It's so common for people to go around in a constant state of stress, always tensed-up and on high alert—and this is so unnecessary. The problem is, most of us aren't even aware that we're holding onto stress. It's handy to have that initial reaction when a car swerves into your lane, but you don't want to let something like that affect your whole day. There are all kinds of simple ways to bring your body back into a relaxed state after the danger is over. Tapping your upper arms alternately is a really easy one.

When we don't release stress, it can wreak havoc on our bodies and our mental state. The first step in breaking the stress cycle is recognizing it. The signs most people experience are usually:

- Tension in the shoulders, neck, or jaw
- Rapid heartbeat
- Shallow breathing
- Digestive issues
- Fatigue
- Headaches
- Brain fog
- Feelings of overwhelm

Once you've identified these signals, you can take action to interrupt the stress response. Deep breathing is a technique you can do any time, even while you're driving. This is as simple as it sounds. Take a slow, deep breath through your nose, filling your belly. Hold for a count of four, then exhale slowly through your mouth. Take five to ten slow, deep breaths in a row. Then allow your body to breathe in whatever way it needs to and check for any residual signs of stress.

To go into a deeper relaxed state. Lie down and close your eyes. Tense your toes for five seconds, then release. Work your way up to your ankles, your legs...all the way up to your neck and then your face. Check in with each part of your body as you relax it to see if it needs further attention.

Both of these techniques are great for releasing stress in the moment. If you find yourself needing to rely on them a lot, it might be time to take a look at your daily habits and see if there are any sources of stress you can eliminate. Keep in mind that it's important to know the difference between situations you can and can't change. There will be some stressors in your life you can't get rid of, and that's normal. Just work within your situation as well as you can.

If regular exercise and meditation are new for you, start by congratulating yourself when you spend one minute in silence or when you park a little farther from the grocery store door. These little beginnings grow into habits that make your body more resistant to stress and your life more enjoyable.

Stress management is a skill that takes awareness and practice. Be patient with yourself as you learn to recognize and respond to your body's signals.

Food and Your Body's Wisdom

What we eat has a huge impact on how we feel, both physically and emotionally. Yet in our busy lives, we tend to eat mindlessly, barely tasting our food, let alone noticing how it makes our bodies feel.

If you feel any discomfort, you may find the solution with a two-week diet diary. You might even try this very thorough plan:

After each meal or snack, jot down three things:

- What you ate, and how much
- How you felt physically after eating it or the next day? (Energized, sluggish, bloated, itchy, etc.)
- Any emotions before or after eating

Most people who do this practice are surprised by what they notice. You might realize that it's harder to think clearly several hours after eating sugar, for example.

To tap into my body's wisdom about food, I kept a food diary for a couple of weeks. I wanted to know what caused headaches and a mysterious pain on my right side. They weren't always there, just once in a while, but why? In order to find out, I recorded what I ate and drank for a couple of weeks.

That was an eye opening experiment! I learned that I could handle vegetable oils, but not if I consumed them two days in a row. Since then I've stopped cooking with highly processed (and quickly rancid) vegetable oils, and my liver is much happier.

Your body is wise. By learning to listen to your body, you can start to uncover and heal some of those old wounds that have been making it so challenging to cherish and care for yourself.

Paying attention to when you eat as well as what you eat can be illuminating too–especially if you have trouble sleeping. I find that cutting myself off from any meals or snacks two or three hours before going to bed makes a big difference. Many people notice that they sleep better after eating a protein-rich meal or complex carbohydrates, as opposed to simple sugars that raise and then drop blood sugar levels. We know from research that there is a direct relationship between depression and sugar consumption.

And whatever other changes you make–always make sure you're drinking enough clean water. So much physical discomfort and even serious conditions can be traced back to lack of hydration.

Mindful Eating

Mindful eating is another way to tune into your body's messages around food. For some people, mindful eating is a whole lifestyle. Many years ago, I learned that I needed to "drink" solid foods and chew liquids in order to have the digestive enzymes in my mouth interact with the food for better digestion and absorption. I'm not asking you to take it that far, at least not right now. As an experiment, just choose a small morsel of food like a raisin or a cracker.

- Hold it in front of your face and observe it with all your senses. Does it look and smell appealing? What does the texture tell you?
- Next, place the food in your mouth, but don't chew it yet. What are your tastebuds telling you? Notice any other new sensations in your mouth and in your body.
- Now you can chew the food. Chew slowly, still paying attention to taste and texture.

- Once the food is thoroughly chewed, you can swallow it. Notice the sensations as it moves down your throat.
- For the next several seconds, sit quietly and notice the sensations, emotions, and thoughts that arise.

This level of attention might feel strange at first, but it's a powerful exercise to reconnect with your body's innate wisdom about food. I am not suggesting that you eat like this all the time. It's just a great practice for times when you want to know whether a particular food is good for your body or not. It has worked well for me.

For example, I was working on this chapter at a cafe and suddenly realized how hungry I was. I ordered an egg salad on a croissant. Bringing all of my awareness to my mouth as I chewed the bread, I realized how oily it was. I usually use avocado and olive oils at home, in part to avoid blemishes. I knew they probably used vegetable oil which is hard on the body. So I decided then I would enjoy the sandwich and choose something else in the future.

Later, as I worked, I found myself scratching a part of my face that is associated with the stomach in traditional Chinese medicine. Sure enough, a blemish popped up the next day!

Brain Integration

Our brains are truly remarkable and it's amazing what they can do. But sometimes, especially under stress, our brains go into survival mode, our thoughts start going in circles, and we end up feeling stuck. Brain integration techniques like the Hook-Ups help both hemispheres of our brain work together more effectively, and each time we practice them it gets a little bit easier to pull ourselves out of those ruts.

Another simple but powerful technique for integrating the brain is the Cross Crawl, as described on the Original Strength blog (originalstrength.net) by Tim Anderson. Here's how to do it:

1. Stand up straight.
2. Lift your right arm and left leg simultaneously.
3. As you lower them, lift your left arm and right leg.
4. Continue this alternating pattern for 1-2 minutes.

This exercise helps coordinate the left and right sides of your brain and body. It can be especially helpful when you're feeling scattered or having trouble focusing. A long walk is great too. The Cross Crawl is like a short walk in place.

By practicing these and other brain integration techniques (Hook-Ups for one!), you're building neural pathways that support whole-brain thinking. This can lead to better decision making, more creative problem solving, and a greater sense of emotional balance in your daily life.

Healing is not a linear process. Each time you show up for yourself in this way, you're reinforcing patterns of self-love and self-care.

Your body is wise. It holds onto memories and emotions that your conscious mind might have forgotten,pushed aside or buried. By learning to listen to your body, you can start to uncover and heal some of those old wounds that have been making it so challenging to cherish and care for yourself.

Body Scan

Here is one way to tune into your body, so that you can recognize where you might be holding onto trapped emotions and begin to create a safe space for those emotions to surface and release.

Find a quiet, comfortable place where you won't be disturbed for about 15-20 minutes. Sit or lie down in a position that feels good for your body.

Take a few deep breaths, allowing your body to relax with each exhale. It can help to imagine roots growing from the base of your spine, anchoring you safely to the Earth.

Now, bring your attention to your body. Start at the top of your head and move down to your toes in a slow body scan. Notice any areas of tension, discomfort, or unusual sensation.

When you find an area that feels tense or uncomfortable, pause there. Without trying to change anything, simply observe the sensation. Is it tight? Achy? Tingly? Hot or cold?

As you focus on this sensation, ask yourself gently: "What emotion might be connected to this physical feeling?" Don't worry if you don't get an immediate answer. Just stay curious.

If an emotion does surface (maybe sadness, anger, fear, or something else), welcome it. Say to it, "I see you. I hear you. You're safe here."

Breathe into that area of your body, imagining that you're creating space around the sensation and the emotion. You're not trying to make it go away, just giving it room to be. If it feels right, you might place a hand on this part of your body, offering yourself comfort and connection.

You can even ask the emotion questions, like, "How long have you been here? What do you need?" Acknowledge what comes up in response to these questions.

Stay with this process for as long as feels comfortable. When you're ready to finish, take a few deep breaths and slowly bring your attention back to the room around you.

Take a moment to jot down any insights or experiences you had during this exercise.

The key is to approach this exercise, and yourself, with gentleness and curiosity. You're not trying to force anything. Some days you might have profound revelations, and other days you might just feel a bit more relaxed. Both are perfectly okay. You're not trying to fix anything; you're simply getting to know yourself better, creating a foundation for deeper self-love and acceptance.

If you find time to do this practice regularly, you might start to notice patterns. Maybe certain emotions always show up in particular parts of your body. Or perhaps you begin to connect current reactions to past experiences. This awareness is the first step in healing and transforming these old patterns.

Healing is not a linear process. Some days will be easier than others. But each time you show up for yourself in this way, you're reinforcing patterns of self-love and self-care. You're teaching your body and your mind that it's safe to feel, safe to heal, and safe to love yourself.

In the next chapter, we'll explore specific techniques for overcoming the resistance that often pops up when we do this deep healing work.

Chapter Seven
Come Home to Your Truth

Remember back in Chapter Four when I told you about believing I was bad for most of my life? I thought my parents sent me to stay with the babysitter when I was a toddler because I was useless. I thought I was unlovable because I was born a girl and not a boy. I believed I was bad for experiencing physical pleasure because after feeling sexual energy, I was hastily tossed back into the playpen bed.

All of these beliefs created by the feelings stuck in my body were dictating my reality by the time I was three years old, and they got more deeply ingrained as time went by. The belief that I was somehow broken or unworthy colored everything I did and every interaction with the people around me. I was miserable as a child. I felt so alone. I know now that my parents loved me immensely, but I couldn't feel it.

One powerful tool for changing our beliefs is the human voice.

I don't remember my kindergarten teacher telling my mother I needed help making friends, but it made sense when I heard the story later. Because I already believed I was bad, I readily took on the belief that friendships would be dangerous because the person would eventually find out how bad I was! When I realized that this didn't have to be my truth, I enthusiastically began making up for lost time developing my social skills. I'm still at it, and I'm getting friendlier all the time!

When we are convinced that something is true, we subconsciously go around looking for evidence to confirm it. And let me tell you, when you're looking for proof that you're bad, you'll find it everywhere, even in the most innocent situations. But I want you to know that no matter how long you've been carrying these beliefs, it's never too late to change them.

I went to see an astrologer when I was in my twenties. He told me my purpose on Earth was to be good. You would think that would make me feel better about myself, right? But no, my mind twisted it around. I didn't believe I was already innately good. That was out of the question. I thought my mission was to *become* good and I went away feeling that obviously, I must be, or have been, bad. "Good" was all I had ever wanted to be, but clearly I was not good enough.

We all have stubborn beliefs like this. Sometimes we're aware of them, sometimes not. Most of them are like programs running in the background of our minds shaping how we see everything. In Chapter Four, I told you that these beliefs can be changed, and I described Ho'oponopono, one of the most powerful tools I know for rewiring our minds so that we can fill them with more loving, joyful, and peaceful thoughts.

For years, I found myself moving from house to house every two to three years, like clockwork. It was just something I did, without ever asking why. It wasn't until I was 50 years old that I learned about the trauma I experienced at the babysitter's house when I was a toddler.

I was too young to understand what was happening, so my body internalized this experience as a belief. I would settle in somewhere, two years would pass, and then for reasons I couldn't explain, it was time to leave. For decades, I kept recreating this pattern in my adult life, moving every two to three years without ever knowing why. Now I realize it had to do with being uprooted from my family and sent to stay with the babysitter when my brother was born.

What a pile of crappy beliefs I have had to dig out from under!

Here's an example from someone else's life. I met a woman whose father was told by the doctor that she was definitely going to be a boy, right up until the day she was born. When she finally arrived, he was so disappointed he turned around and walked out of the hospital. Her parents hadn't even chosen a girl's name.

It takes a conscious effort to allow ourselves to be surprised by a different view.

Her father's name was Gene, and she was supposed to be Gene Jr. Instead, she was named Jean. Jean and her father butted heads all her life. She grew up believing two things about men: one that they would argue about everything and two that they would eventually turn their backs and walk away from her. When, as an adult, she heard the story about her

(...) These beliefs are not facts about who you are. They're only thoughts you've practiced thinking over and over again.

father's disappointment at her birth, she realized where these beliefs came from.

This is what I mean when I talk about conditioning. We all carry unconscious beliefs that were formed by experiences we may not even remember. Although these beliefs may have been formed long before we were old enough to think them through, they continue to distort our reality until we recognize them, challenge them, and dismantle them.

How did your own early experiences shape your experiences now? Are there any patterns you would like to break free from? If you don't remember much about your early childhood or don't know the story of your birth, is there anyone you can ask?

Once you've identified your own limiting beliefs, there are practical steps you can take to change them. These techniques have helped me, my clients, and many friends over the years to replace those old, harmful beliefs about ourselves and cultivate thoughts that are kinder and more appreciative of our innate goodness.

Let's start by looking at some of the beliefs you have about yourself. Don't worry if you can't immediately identify any deep-seated ones. For now, just think about how you talk to yourself in your head. I would like you to consider these three questions.

1. **What do you say to yourself when you make a mistake?**

Do you berate yourself or give yourself space to try again? Do you acknowledge difficulties that are not your fault, or do you blame yourself for things outside of your control?

2. How do you feel when you look in the mirror?

Do you greet your reflection with a warm smile? Or do you stare yourself down, looking for flaws? Do you look away quickly or allow yourself to enjoy a moment of self-admiration? Does that last suggestion sound audacious to you? (So many of us women were raised not to find joy in our own physical nature.)

3. What thoughts come up when you're faced with a challenge?

Do you give yourself a mental pep talk? Do you speak affirmations with a strong confident voice? Do you prepare for success or brace against failure?

If you're not sure how to answer these questions, watch your mind in action as you go through your day. Stop and reflect on the thoughts that start running through your mind next time you make a mistake, look in the mirror, or set out to do something challenging. Do you notice any thoughts you would like to change? Do any beliefs come to the surface that might not be completely accurate?

You Can Change Your Filter

We each live in our own personal reality. I'm not saying that what you experience in your own reality isn't real—it's just that it's incomplete. Our eyes, ears, skin, noses, and taste buds take in way more sensory information than our brains can process all at once, so we filter it.

Our thoughts are like seeds we plant in the garden of our minds. What we focus on grows, so it's crucial to nurture loving thoughts and weed out the negative ones.

There's an easy way to prove this. Think about the last time you went to a movie with other people. After the film, you probably talked about what you'd just seen. Did everyone have exactly the same take on the story? Chances are, each person noticed different details, connected more strongly with different characters, or interpreted the themes in their own unique way.

This isn't because you each saw a different movie. You all sat in the same theater, watching the same screen. But each of you filtered that shared experience through your own personal lens.

Two people can be in the same meeting and come away with very different impressions of what was said. A couple can share a conversation and later disagree about what was actually discussed. It's not that one person is right and the other is wrong. They're each experiencing our own filtered version of reality.

The lenses through which we see the world are always going to be tinted by our expectations based on our past experiences. When we see only what we expect to see, the view naturally gets pretty distorted. It takes a conscious effort to allow ourselves to be surprised by a different view.

When you realize that your perception isn't the whole truth, but just one possible interpretation filtered through your own beliefs and experiences, it becomes easier to be gentle with yourself. You can start to question those negative beliefs about yourself, recognizing that they're not absolute truths, but just one possible way of seeing things.

So next time you catch yourself thinking negative thoughts about yourself, ask yourself: Is this the only way to see this situation? What other interpretations might be possible? By opening yourself up to other perspectives, you create space for more loving, compassionate views of yourself and your experiences.

You can practice this by choosing one challenging interaction or situation from your day. Take a few quiet minutes to sit comfortably, close your eyes, and mentally place yourself in the other person's physical position. Notice what the scene looks like from where they were standing or sitting. What were they seeing when they looked at you? Gently breathe into their experience. What emotions come up?

What pressures were they under? What fears or hopes might have been driving their actions? I entered a childhood memory of watching my mother go over my dad's accounts for his repair business, then I looked at the situation through her eyes. She was trained in office skills and had purchased a fancy journal to track his income and expenses. When I saw how entries stopped after a few months, I suddenly understood her fear of not having enough money to feed us.

In another situation, viewing a work conflict through a colleague's perspective helped me see how overwhelmed they had been with family problems at home. This simple practice of imagining ourselves in another's position, even for a few minutes, can transform old hurts into understanding and help us respond with more compassion in the moment.

It is valuable to remind ourselves to capture moments to celebrate ourselves.

Once you start examining long-held beliefs, you will find that most of them are pretty out of date! Congratulate yourself for discovering them. Most were formed in early childhood, when your understanding of the world was pretty incomplete.

I spent a lifetime gathering evidence that I was "bad." Along the way, I passed up all kinds of clues that I actually have some pretty decent qualities and that I am worthy of love and respect.

Every so often, something would happen that made it impossible to ignore that I was actually a good person inside. I was at a seminar where the instructor had us do a guided imagery exercise. We were supposed to visualize the light within ourselves. And you know what? I actually saw it!

For the first time in my life, I had a glimpse of my own inner light, my innate goodness. It was a real thing! I couldn't deny it anymore—I was already fulfilling the purpose that the astrologer had seen in me all those decades ago. My negative belief about myself was just that—a belief. It wasn't the truth about who I was.

Another clue that those beliefs I'd held onto for so long were off the mark was when I had a brief relationship with a man in a spiritual community who truly saw me, cherished me, and wanted to nurture me. I was able to look at myself through his eyes, and his vision of me was more real than anything I had ever felt. I couldn't stop crying. I wasn't ready to receive such caring devotion at the time, but the feeling has always stuck with me.

Now, I'm not saying you need to start going to seminars or get someone to fall in love with you to see that you are worthy of love. You can see it anywhere, any time. The trick is simply to look for it and allow yourself to see.

What Do You Believe About Yourself Now?

Take a moment to write down the first three beliefs that come into your head. They could be positive or negative. For example, you might write "I'm not good enough," "I'm always late," or "I'm a kind person." Don't overthink it. Just write down the first three beliefs that come to mind.

Now, look at what you've written for question 10 on the Self-Love Quiz in Chapter Two. Can you remember when you first started believing these things about yourself? Was there a specific event or person that influenced these beliefs? Or have they just always been there, as far as you can remember?

Know that just because you've believed something for a long time doesn't mean it's true. These beliefs are not facts about who you are. They're only thoughts you've practiced thinking over and over again. And just like we can practice thinking negative thoughts, we can also practice thinking more loving, supportive thoughts about ourselves.

Sing Your Way to a New Reality

One powerful tool for changing our beliefs is the human voice, particularly when we're singing. I'll give you an example of how I use this tool.

I have struggled with chronic lateness. I thought it was just part of who I was—another one of the flaws that I couldn't stop seeing in myself. I discovered a possible reason–my dad was sent home from the hospital because I took so long to be born. I would leave late sometimes when I was supposed to be there and wanted to move as quickly as possible on the freeway where I lived. I had learned about the power of our thought and I knew that if I kept thinking I'm late I'm late I would only be more late. I created a song that made me think of arriving on time:

"I arrive! I arrive! I arri—ii—iiiiiive! I arrive in the perfect time!"

I sang this ditty in an exaggerated Scottish/Irish accent, which required my full attention to get the accent right. This took my focus away from the repetitive self-critical thoughts about being late.

It worked! I would stop thinking that I was going to be late and I saw openings in the traffic where I was able to pass slower cars, saving precious minutes.

Vibrating our vocal cords through singing and humming stimulates the vagus nerve, which is the largest part of the parasympathetic nervous system. This calms the physical body so that the organs work better, and it enhances our feelings.

So if you're working to change a negative belief about yourself, consider creating a simple, catchy tune. Don't worry about musical perfection. If you could hear me singing some of the songs I go around singing to myself throughout the day, you would probably laugh—which would be good for you and me both!

When you sing a positive message to yourself, you're not just thinking it, you're feeling it in your whole body. When you speak or sing, you can feel the vibrations in your chest, your throat, even in your bones. It's a way of physically shaking loose those old, stuck beliefs and making space for new, happier ones—like you're giving yourself a big, musical hug! If hugging yourself sounds odd, hugging yourself with your voice must sound even farther out there. But just try it. The more you practice, the more natural it will become.

On top of all that, singing releases bliss-inducing endorphins so the positive beliefs we're forming are associated with joy. When you sing your new thoughts about yourself into being, you're linking them to the positive emotions you generate, making your new habits of thought that much stronger.

You don't have to be a great singer for this to work. It's not about how you sound to other people. So go ahead, make up a silly song about how awesome you are. Sing it off-key. Sing it in the shower, in your car, while you're doing the dishes. You might feel a bit foolish at first, but I promise you, it's a lot more fun than beating yourself up. And who knows? You might just sing your way into a kinder, more compassionate and forgiving way of living with the one person you might as well get along with since you'll never have a moment without her!

Mirror Mirror

This next method might make you squirm at first, but it is powerful. I learned about this from Louise Hay's books, and it's been a game-changer for me and many of my clients. Stand in front of a mirror. Any mirror will do, but a full-length one is best if you have it. Look yourself in the eyes and say something kind or appreciative to yourself. Speak to yourself by name. It might feel awkward at first, but stick with it. If you can practice this every day for just one week, I bet you will start to notice a difference in how you feel toward yourself.

You could start with something simple like, "You are a good person, Martha," if Martha is your name. Or you might want to address a specific belief you're working on changing. For example, if you wrote down "I'm not good enough" as one of your beliefs about yourself, you could say to your reflection, "You are more than good enough. You are worthy and valuable just as you are."

You might not believe what you're saying at first. That's okay. As long as it feels possible, stick with it and you can make your new belief come true.

I remember the first time I tried this. I stood in front of my bathroom mirror, looked at myself, and tried to say, "I love you, Linda." I couldn't even get the words out! I couldn't relate to those words. I didn't want to think of how long I'd gone without showing myself any kindness or love.

I kept at it, though. Every day, I'd look in that mirror and say something nice to myself. Some days it was just, "Hey, you're doing okay." Other days, I could manage a full "I love you." And bit by bit, it got easier.

A friend of mine had only been practicing this for about two weeks before her partner started telling her the same compliments she was giving herself in the mirror! And no, he didn't overhear her practicing.

One last thing about this practice: when you greet yourself in the mirror, remember to smile. Even if it feels fake, your body will still release feel-good chemicals. If it feels weird to be saying nice things to yourself, remind yourself as often as you need to that this isn't about being vain. You're simply treating yourself with the same kindness and respect you'd offer a good friend.

Your Thoughts are the Seeds of Your Reality

Our thoughts are like seeds we plant in the garden of our minds. What we focus on grows, so it's crucial to nurture loving thoughts and weed out the negative ones. The mother of one of my childhood friends used to tell her children as they were leaving the house, "Be on the lookout for something good in your day." At dinner she would ask what good things they found. You can say the same thing to yourself as you go out your front door in the morning, and then recall the goodness you experienced each day as you sit down to dinner.

Another way to cultivate positive thoughts about yourself is to learn to do something new. Choose something fun so the challenge is worth it, not so difficult that you will spend a lot of time in frustration. Bonus points if learning this new activity means connecting with a new group of people! It's important to spend time with people who enjoy life and are excited to grow with you.

As best you can, avoid spending time with people who criticize themselves–those thought patterns are contagious.

Celebrate Yourself

It's wonderful when we celebrate ourselves on our birthdays. But why wait a whole year to acknowledge how special we are? We're worth celebrating more often than that!

I remember meeting a family who had a beautiful practice. They created their own personal holidays throughout the year, celebrating special events in the family's experience: like the day Billy caught the big fish. Or when Sis hit her grand slam that won the game. This idea stuck with me. I thought, "Why can't we do this for ourselves?" We can celebrate our special days of success every year. We don't need to wait for others to celebrate us. We can create our own rituals of self-appreciation.

It is valuable to remind ourselves to capture moments to celebrate ourselves. Whether it is small scale, daily acts of self-love, or taking a whole day just for yourself, we need to make time for ourselves. I like to do the things I love in the small moments between tasks. I have to remember to ask myself, "What would feel good right now?" Sometimes it feels good to go on a walk or listen to music. I like getting cozy in a jacket on a cold day and going on a walk to enjoy nature. After a while, these practices start to become a habit. The important thing is that you're consciously setting aside time to honor and appreciate yourself.

Or perhaps you create a daily ritual, like that family did. Every evening, look back on the dayand see how many things you can find to celebrate. I know there will be at least a few, even if they are small. Maybe you caught negative thoughts in the morning before they spiraled into a bad mood. Maybe you set up a system to make watering your plants easier.

The point is to regularly remind yourself that you and the life you are living is worthy of celebration, not just once a year on your birthday, but every single day. Because you are unique, valuable, and deserving of love and appreciation—especially from yourself.

We've explored how to nurture and respect our bodies and how to take charge of our thoughts. Now it's time to dive even deeper, into the wellspring of wisdom that resides in your heart. Our minds are powerful tools which keep our bodies safe and operating, but they can also lead us astray with endless chatter and worry. Your heart, on the other hand, holds a different kind of intelligence—one that's connected to your deepest truths and intuitions.

Chapter Eight
Come Home to Your Heart

As I shared with you earlier in this book, I wasn't exactly what you would call a happy child. Remember how I told you about that time when the Beatles first appeared on TV singing "All My Loving"? While my family and friends were crowded around the set, I retreated to my room and closed the door. That's how uncomfortable I was with expressions of love and happiness.

I had moments of joy riding my bike and water skiing behind my dad's boat. Those were rare moments when I was able to comfortably inhabit my body, and those times only happened when I was alone.

Allowing ourselves to experience beauty and joy in life isn't some luxurious reward, it's essential!

One night stands out from every other childhood memory because it was a taste of joy that I experienced through connecting with other people. It was Halloween, and

I was 13 years old and going to a party. I dressed up as a fortune teller, complete with my grandmother's rose globe as my crystal ball.

Kids came up to me, curious about my costume and the globe. So, without really thinking about it, I started "reading fortunes" for them.

At the time I didn't know about psychic abilities, and I had no training in gathering information intuitively. But as I imagined seeing each person in the glass sphere, I found that I was actually sensing things about them. Words of encouragement rolled off my tongue. With each pronouncement, I felt better and better.

To my surprise, I didn't feel any anxiety. I wasn't self-conscious at all. All I felt was joy! I was a part of that party, fully connected and sharing the experience with everyone else who was there. For once, I wasn't worrying about how others saw me or whether I was saying the wrong things. I wasn't trying to make myself invisible. I was fully present and, dare I say it, having fun.

I was connecting to my heart, that part of us that feels joy, pain, love, and everything in between. People mean a variety of different things when they talk about the heart, like they do when they talk about love. In this chapter, I'm not talking about the physical heart that pumps blood. I'm not talking about the metaphysical heart yet either—that's coming up in the next chapter. This chapter is about the part of our being that feels emotions, tunes into the experience of others, and forms those blissful connections that we call love.

In whatever ways you've limited your own ability to feel joy (we all do it!) I hope you'll find in this chapter the encouragement you need to open your heart to love and connection—whatever that feels like in each moment.

It was many years before I felt that blissful feeling of connection again the way I did at that Halloween party. Like so many women, I was uncomfortable with the idea of seeking out pleasure and joy. We go through life believing we shouldn't be happy because we haven't done anything to earn it. We think pleasure will somehow spoil us. We punish ourselves needlessly.

I've learned that allowing ourselves to experience beauty and joy in life isn't some luxurious reward, it's essential! A big part of loving yourself is nurturing your heart's capacity to feel whatever it needs to feel.

For a long time, I struggled with the idea that I deserved to have nice things, or that it was ok to use the nice things that I already had. I'd buy a pricey vitamin supplement and then not use it because I would have to buy more. I'd wear stained T-shirts for pajamas, telling myself, "no one can see them anyway." Underlying this was a feeling that if I didn't cost money, I would be loved. My parents were born during the Great Depression and they budgeted well. My dad proudly told me that the only thing they ever bought on time was my mother's sewing machine and they paid that off with a loan from the bank. Conserving money made me feel safe.

We might tell ourselves to "just get over it" or "look on the bright side." But denying these emotions pushes them deeper inside where they can cause problems later.

A turning point came when a friend gave me a beautiful, hand-thrown mug as a gift. At first, I was reluctant to use it.

I didn't want to break it. I put it away, telling myself that I would use it on "special occasions."

A year went by, and no occasion seemed special enough. I almost forgot I had that mug. When I found it again in the back of the cupboard, I felt sad about the lack of appreciation I had been showing for my friend's gift. I poured my first cup of tea into the mug that day, and from then on, I allowed myself to use it on a regular basis. Using that mug every morning, starting my days with something beautiful, became a small act of self-love. Even the smallest acts of self-love can help us overcome those deep-seated feelings of unworthiness that so many of us carry.

You Deserve to Enjoy Your Life

Think about your own life. Are there ways you're denying yourself simple pleasures or comforts? How often do you stop yourself from doing something that brings you joy? Maybe you tell yourself you don't have the time or the money, or that it's frivolous, or that you should be doing something more productive, something that serves others instead of yourself.

Have you ever walked by the flower department of your grocery store and had the impulse to treat yourself to a bouquet or a single flower? If you're like most women, you probably didn't act on it. I was impressed when a woman I used to visit told me that the beautiful bouquets that graced her kitchen table, week after week, were her own gift to herself. I was inspired and learned which flowers lasted the longest so I could be economical AND show myself that I was loved and deserved to have a home graced by the natural beauty of flowers. I have been told that looking at a flower when you're upset can shift your energy. I tried it and it worked. Watching squirrels chasing each other in the maple tree outside my patio door has also moved me into a state of joy.

How about trying an experiment? The next time you feel drawn to something beautiful—a sunset, a piece of music, the laughter of a child—give yourself permission to stop and fully experience it. Take a deep breath and simply be present with that moment of beauty.

And go ahead and treat yourself to whatever small pleasure you've been denying yourself. Put your good sheets on the bed just because you want to. Play the music you love. Rearrange the furniture the way you like it. Set aside time each day to take yourself for a walk in nature.

Do these things especially if you feel you don't deserve them. Because when we constantly deny ourselves the small pleasures in life, we're sending a message to our hearts that joy isn't important. Over time, this can lead to a kind of emotional numbness. If you've been numb for a while, opening yourself up to joy again will be uncomfortable at first. Stick with it, and you might be pleasantly surprised at how much joy can grow and spread in your life just by engaging in one simple pleasure at a time. I feel great joy when I get a smile from someone like a clerk, a parent or a child when I compliment them on doing something well.

Experience the Full Range of Emotions

As important as it is to allow ourselves to feel joy and happiness, it's equally valuable to acknowledge and work through our more uncomfortable emotions too. Many of us have been taught to push aside feelings like sadness, anger, or fear. We might tell ourselves to "just get over it" or "look on the bright side." But denying these emotions doesn't make them go away—it just pushes them deeper inside where they can fester and cause problems later. The average daily emotions are useful feedback tools, telling us that something is not quite right. If we step back and notice what prompted an emotional response, we can learn a lot. In Chapter Six, where I wrote about the different types of messages we can receive from our bodies when we ground ourselves in our physical experience, I talked about how so many of the aches and pains we feel can alert us to buried emotions that we need to process.

When I was growing up, emotions were usually dismissed. We couldn't see them or grab hold of them, so we didn't think we had to experience them. We believed we could ignore them and they would go away.

Healing emotional wounds isn't going to be a once-and-done process, so be patient with yourself.

We now know that reality doesn't have to have a material form to matter! Thanks to the work of neuroscientists, we know that our emotional experiences actually change the structure and functioning of our brains. What this means is that your emotions are very real, and the stress of burying them can cause real physical changes in our brains and bodies. It can weaken our immune systems, increase inflammation, and even change our DNA. Trauma and prolonged stress have everything to do with how we experience reality going forward, no matter how much we try to leave them in the past.

That's why taking care of emotional health is a big part of self-love.

When I realized this, it changed my approach to healing as a chiropractor. I started using a reliable technique called muscle testing to get "yes" or "no" answers when I directly asked a client's body what the root cause of their pain was. When I ask a client's body the age at which a similar emotion surfaced for the first time, more often than not, the painful memory of an old emotional wound would surface. This is because our bodies hold onto our emotions until we're ready to process them.

Once we identified these old emotional patterns, we would use a method I call "growing up" the belief. It was like giving their adult self a chance to comfort and reassure that hurt child within them. I found that when the child was willing to be comforted by the adult, the client recovered faster.

One example was a client who came to me with severe back pain. As we worked together, it became clear that her physical discomfort had everything to do with an emotional problem she didn't want to face. Her father was very ill, and she was struggling with the possibility of losing him. She told me, "If he dies, he will never be able to tell me that he loves me!" Once she had articulated this, the floodgates opened. She made peace with the fact that expressing love in words was something her father could not bring himself to do, and her back pain eased.

Healing deep emotional pain takes courage, but it's so worth it.

I recommend always combining a caring action toward yourself with painful feelings that come up. Do something simple like place your hand on your heart when you feel sad, or take a few deep breaths when you feel anxious. These small, compassionate gestures let your heart, mind and body know that you will be cared for and protected as you heal. Here are some other simple approaches I've found effective:

Feel it to heal it. Give yourself permission to fully experience your emotions without judgment. This might mean setting aside time to cry, to feel angry, or to sit with your fear. It's not about wallowing, but about giving your feelings the space they need to be processed.

Reach out. Talk to a trusted friend, join a support group, or see a therapist. Sharing your emotions with others can be incredibly healing. It helps us feel less alone and can give us new ways of looking at our experiences.

Be kind to yourself. When difficult emotions come up, try talking to yourself the way you'd talk to someone you love when they're going through a tough time.

Use mind-body techniques. Meditation, yoga, and simple deep breathing exercises can help release emotions stored in the body. Remember that these techniques don't need to be complicated in order to work. Just one minute of mindfulness meditation will noticeably calm your mind. Let your body guide you.

Write it out. Journaling about our experiences and feelings can help us process them more effectively. It's amazing what insights can come through when we get our thoughts out of our heads and onto paper!

Get creative. Art, music, dance, or any other form of creativity can be a powerful outlet for emotions that are hard to put into words.

Healing emotional wounds isn't going to be a once-and-done process, so be patient with yourself each time emotions you thought you had already dealt with come to the surface. The idea isn't to erase the past or get to a point where you're no longer susceptible to feeling pain. Life on Earth is messy, things will continue to go wrong, and there will always be some elements of sadness and fear. What you are learning is to move through your feelings—all kinds of feelings—in a healthier way so that you can return to a state of joy more easily each time.

It's easy to feel happy when everything's going right, when you're sitting in the sun on a beautiful day without a care in the world. But then an unexpected bill arrives, your computer crashes, or someone says something that hurts your feelings. There's no end to the things that can interrupt our happiness if we let them.

By embracing all your emotions, both the difficult ones and the happy ones, you're taking care of your heart, and you're keeping your mind and body healthy too.

For a long time, I would let these little setbacks spiral me into a bad mood that could last for hours or even days. But I've learned that we can train ourselves to respond differently. We can reset our emotions after they signal us that something is wrong according to our current beliefs.

The key is knowing that so many of our reactions are based on beliefs that were programmed into us before we were old enough to understand what was happening. Our brains are wired to focus on what can go wrong more than what's going right. This goes back to the way our early ancestors survived on the savannah—if there's a lion stalking you, you want to be aware of the situation. Fortunately, we can choose to retrain our brains to focus on the positive and our hearts and bodies will create more of what's good in the world.

I remember one day I was at the library, working on my computer. Something wasn't going right, and I could feel myself getting more and more frustrated. But this time, after a few minutes, I caught myself. "No!" I said to myself, "This is not the feeling you want to experience right now. You don't want to attract more of this into your day!" So I stopped what I was doing, took a deep breath, and told myself, "Time to do something else!"

This is what I call a reset. Breathe deeply with your eyes closed. Shift your position, or stand up and move if you're sitting. Go get a glass of water. Just like that, you can stop a downward spiral before it really gets going.

One of my favorite breathwork practices is great for resetting emotions. It's called Candle Breath. Inhale deeply, then exhale with gentle, directed force as if blowing out a candle. Do this a few times. Then visualize energy flowing up from the Earth through your feet and out the top of your head and down around your body like a fountain.

The goal isn't necessarily to fix the problem right away, but to interrupt the cycle of negative thoughts and emotions so you can think clearly about your options. You always have options. The key is to catch yourself early. Stay grounded in your body so that you can notice as soon as you're starting to get upset.

One of my favorite ways to reset is to get out in nature. There's something about being around trees, or near water, or just feeling the sun on my face that helps me ground myself and put things in perspective.

Accept What's Coming to You

Remember to enjoy the good times too! It's too easy to let happy moments slip by without much thought. We're so busy worrying about tomorrow or rehashing yesterday that we miss out on the joy right in front of us.

Here's something I've found helpful: At the end of each day, I think of three good things that happened. They don't have to be anything huge. Maybe it was a beautiful sunset, a dog that came up to me for a scratch, or finding fresh ginger at the local farmers market. I take a moment to really relive those experiences. How did they make me feel? What did I notice in my body?

If you make a habit of regularly engaging with happy memories, it will help train your mind to spot and appreciate life's little joys. Over time, you might find yourself noticing more good moments as they happen. Think of this practice as building a reserve of happy memories that can lift your spirits when times get tough.

By embracing all your emotions, both the difficult ones and the happy ones, you're taking care of your heart, and you're keeping your mind and body healthy too.

Opening a Closed Heart

Sometimes, despite our best intentions, we find our hearts closed and connection seems impossible. We've been hurt before and we're afraid of becoming vulnerable again. We've fallen into unhealthy habits in our thinking and our emotions are spiraling.

Here are some common symptoms of a closed heart:

- Feeling defensive or irritable
- Exhaustion and lack of inspiration
- Feeling disconnected from others and yourself
- Difficulty feeling or expressing love
- Loss of spontaneity
- Holding your breath or shallow breathing
- Lack of participation in life

I experienced this myself when the man I had met in college and fallen in love with ended our relationship. For a long time, I just went through the motions of going to work in the morning and then straight home in the afternoon. There was a community center just a block away offering classes and activities that normally would have interested me, but I didn't go. My heart was closed.

If you recognize these signs in yourself, don't give up, you are more clever than those old patterns. Love yourself through it, and you will find in yourself your own best friend.

There are many ways to gently open a closed heart. Here are few:

Move your body to music. Even if you don't feel like it, put on your favorite upbeat songs and let yourself dance freely. This helps release tension and connects you to joy.

Laugh. Watch funny movies or cartoons. Laughter is a powerful way to open the heart.

Connect with animals. Play with a pet or spend time around animals. Their unconditional love can be healing.

Sing your affirmations. Don't just tell yourself you're worthy of love. Singing opens your throat chakra, inviting your authentic self to come out to play. It also helps form new neural pathways to help positive thought patterns take hold. So sing out loud!

Celebrate small victories. Have you taken a risk lately? Stood up for something you believe in? Completed a difficult task? Acknowledge the goodness in your heart and celebrate!

Forgive. It's impossible to open your heart when you're carrying a grudge. Recognized that everyone makes mistakes and everyone has the capacity to grow. Practice Ho'Oponopono when you want to forgive people who have let you down, including yourself. And then forgive yourself for holding things against them!

Physically open your chest area. Yoga poses that expand the chest, like backbends, cobra pose, warrior pose, and bridge pose, can physically and energetically open the heart.

You can also open your heart through your nose using the aromas of bergamot and rose essential oils.

Chapter Nine
Come Home to Your Spirit

Remember that Halloween story I shared in Chapter Eight? That night when I dressed up as a fortune teller and felt like I was fully part of something for the first time? Looking back, I realize why that experience was so powerful.

As I described in Chapter Four, I felt like I was ostracized by my parents when my brother was born. Since then, I had been going through life as a little castaway, looking for reasons people didn't want me around. That party was the first time I felt like I belonged. People saw me and valued me. I had a role to play that people understood and wanted—and I wasn't just play-acting with my crystal ball.

When we take care of our whole selves, the full picture of who we were meant to be becomes crystal-clear.

When I was "reading fortunes" for the other kids, what I was really doing was seeing the best in them and helping them see it too. I was connecting with

Love can be a verb—an action we take, a choice we make. It can also be a noun—a force that moves through us and between us.

others in a meaningful way, using my soul's natural gifts. I was experiencing my life's purpose. No wonder I felt so good!

Positive emotions have powerful health effects, and there is no more powerful feeling than the joy that comes with knowing we are exactly who we need to be—a unique expression of the divine creative force of the universe.

When we take care of our whole selves—our physical bodies, the thoughts we nurture in our minds, and our emotional wellbeing, the full picture of who we were meant to be becomes crystal-clear.

Experiences like that Halloween party, times when we feel lit up from the inside, can be like a trail of breadcrumbs that lead us to an understanding of our special purpose on this planet. For me, that party was just a hint of what was to come. It took many more years before I fully stepped into my purpose as a healer and guide. But looking back, I can see how that moment was an early signpost, the first of many now that I look back on my life, showing me the way to the joy that comes from using my gifts.

Your gifts are different from mine. You will have to follow your own heart to find out what they are. Think about the times in your life when you've felt most alive, most yourself. What were you doing? Who were you with? These memories can be valuable clues about what gives your life meaning.

The Greatest Feeling Is Love

Love isn't merely a nice idea or a fleeting feeling. It's not just something we give away out of a sense of obligation, whether we feel like it or not.

Love can be a verb—an action we take, a choice we make. It can also be a noun—a force that moves through us and between us. But for most, love is essentially a powerful feeling. It's an emotion so big that when it grows within us, it can't be contained by our physical bodies. It pushes against our edges, reminding us that there's more to us than flesh and bone. Love brings us back to our spiritual nature.

We saw in Chapter Eight how impactful emotions can be, and love is the most potent emotion of all. If you think about it, nothing is more painful than being deprived of the love we need—orphaned infants who don't receive touch don't survive! And at the other end of the spectrum, in a cancer study with rabbits, when all of the other rabbits had toxic organs, one rabbit continued to be healthy. It was discovered that one of the laboratory assistants had taken that rabbit out of its cage and petted it regularly. Nothing is more beautiful than opening our whole beings up to be filled with love. When we do, we know on every level that there is no real separation between ourselves and the rest of the universe. We suddenly remember that we are an essential part of all that exists.

When you experience that you're part of this magnificent, ever-expanding universe, you start to see yourself differently.

This interconnectedness isn't just a beautiful idea. It's a reality that can manifest in surprising ways. Let me share a story that really drove this point home for me.

My friend Michelle had a life-changing experience that blurred the lines between the physical and spiritual realms. She was in a terrible motorcycle accident on a freeway. The crash was so severe that she suffered burst organs and multiple broken bones. To escape the intense pain, Michelle left her body.

In this out-of-body state, she encountered a tall black man with a distinctive mustache and kind eyes. He urged her, "You need to go back to your body. Your kids are going to need you."

Michelle resisted, thinking her sister could care for her children. But the man insisted, "No, you have to go back! Nobody's going to be there for your kids if you don't."

Michelle followed his urging and returned to her broken body. A year later, she was watching TV with her husband when he exclaimed, "Michelle, you're as white as a China doll!" They were watching a program about a man who had driven off Highway 101 in California into the ocean. The man on TV was saying that when he left his body he saw an olive-skinned lady with short, dark hair. Michelle recognized her Italian self. When the camera panned to the man telling the story, it was a tall black guy with a mustache, the same man who had urged her to return to her body!

What's more, their accidents had happened on the same day, at the same time, just in different parts of the country. Michelle later contacted the man through the TV station and they celebrated their good fortunes.

This experience showed me that we are so much more than just our physical bodies. We are, in a very real sense, spiritual beings having a human experience. Even as we live our day-to-day lives, we may be acting in the spiritual realm in ways we might not fully understand.

This is the kind of expanded awareness and connection that love opens us up to. When we embrace love fully—love for ourselves, for others, for all of creation—we open ourselves to experiences and connections that transcend our usual understanding of reality.

You are Not Just You

For the longest time, I struggled with the idea that I was part of something bigger. It seemed too grand, too important for little old me. But once I experienced that reality in my body and in my heart as well as in my mind, everything changed.

Imagine standing on a beach, watching the waves roll in. Each wave is unique, rising and falling in its own time. But step back, and what do you see? A vast, interconnected ocean. That's us. We're the waves, and we're the ocean too.

When I finally understood that I wasn't just Linda, this separate person bumbling through life, but a vital part of all creation, it was like someone flipped a switch inside me. Suddenly, I saw the divine spark in everything! It was there in the trees outside my window,

Find some other way to expand your view, even if it's just in your imagination.

in the stranger smiling at me on the street, and yes, even in myself when I looked in the mirror.

This isn't just some airy-fairy concept. When you experience that you're part of this magnificent, ever-expanding universe, you start to see yourself differently. You realize that just like the universe is constantly creating new stars and galaxies, you too are a creator.

Every thought you think, every word you speak, every action you take—you're creating your reality. It's a big responsibility, sure, but it's also incredibly empowering. I remember the day this really sunk in for me. It was just an ordinary day. Nothing special was going on. I was standing at the sink washing dishes when I realized that even in this simple act, I was creating. I was creating a clean, beautiful space in my home. I was creating order out of chaos. Seeing myself this way brought a rush of serene joy like nothing I had ever experienced. And in that moment, I felt connected to the creative force of the entire universe.

Now, I'm not saying that understanding this will suddenly make all your problems disappear. But it does change how you approach those problems. When you know you're a creator, you stop seeing yourself as a victim of circumstance. Instead, you start asking yourself, "Okay, how can I create a solution here?"

Seeing myself as a creator has helped me in ways I never expected.

Seeing that I am a part of this grand, loving universe, it became clear that I was connected simply because I existed. Just like every star in the sky has its place and purpose, so do I. So do you.

It's like that song I sang as a kid on my bike. "My dear loving Angel, I forgive you!" I didn't fully understand it then, but the angel in that song was me. I was loved and forgiven. I now see that I was intuiting, or angels were sharing, this truth even back then. We are all divine sparks, all creators. And forgiving ourselves—fully accepting and loving ourselves, is key to tapping into this creative power.

Next time you're feeling small or unworthy, try stepping outside. Literally step outside into the great outdoors if you can, go to a window, or find some other way to expand your view, even if it's just in your imagination. Look up at the sky, then look down at the Earth beneath your feet. Feel your feet on the ground and remember that you're standing on a planet spinning through a vast, beautiful universe of galaxies filled with stars and planets, each one unique. Take a deep breath and remember that you are part of all of this. This simple act of imagination can shift your perspective and open you to a deeper wisdom.

You are a creator, just like the force that set the stars in motion. Let that sink in. Feel it in your body. And then ask yourself, "What beautiful thing do I want to create today?"

Body, Mind and Heart Knowing

Now, we can understand these truths in different ways. We can know with our minds that we are not separate from the cosmos and that we are powerful creators. We can hear about the power of love in a seminar, and we can nod and say, "Yes, I believe we're all connected." Hearing this truth from teachers and reading it in books was resonant enough

Small moments of awareness right in the middle of our busy lives is all it takes to come back to who we really are.

for me that I went on a lifelong quest to experience it firsthand. Having felt disconnected my entire life, I wanted to experience on every level that what these wise ones were saying was true.

We can momentarily experience the oneness of all things in our bodies, like I did riding my bike with the fresh wind blowing on my face. And skimming across a mirror-still lake on skis behind my dad's boat. I didn't know how to articulate it at the time, but I, as a spiritual being, was having the joyful experience of being fully embodied on Earth. Those simple moments are among my most blissful memories. Every cell in my body was alive and singing in harmony with every atom in the universe.

But feeling that oneness in our hearts? That's a whole different experience. It's like the difference between seeing a picture of a rain puddle and diving into an ocean.

When we open our hearts to love, we're tapping into the very essence of who we are. Love is what we were meant to experience, to be, and do on this Earth.

This is why feeling our emotions deeply and fully—the entire range of them—is so important. When we allow ourselves to give and receive love without holding back, we remember who we really are. We experience what it means that we are spiritual beings momentarily embodied in this beautiful world.

So as you go forward, I encourage you to open your heart to love. Let yourself feel it fully, in all its joy and sometimes in its pain too. Every time you do, you're expanding your sense of self and spreading joy.

Get to Know That Still Small Voice

It's easy to get caught up in the hustle of daily life and forget what our true nature is. We rush from one task to the next, often feeling like we're just barely keeping our heads above water. But what if I told you that deep within you is a bottomless source of wisdom and peace that you can access any time? This is the wisdom of your heart, and finding it doesn't require hours of meditation or a retreat to a mountaintop. Small moments of awareness right in the middle of our busy lives is all it takes to come back to who we really are.

Our hearts know things our minds can't figure out. They speak to us as tingling energy, in the language of emotions, in sudden inspirations, and in that sense of rightness we get when we're making things a little more beautiful around us. Learning to listen to this inner wisdom takes practice, but it's worth it.

The alarm you set will help you create a habit that you can practice anywhere, any time.

When we tap into what our hearts know, we are stepping back and seeing a bigger picture, which gives us a sense of peace that makes it easier to act out of wisdom and love instead of fear or need. We notice the good in situations we thought were all bad. We find creative solutions to problems that seemed unsolvable.

These small moments of connection can gradually transform how we see ourselves and our lives. We begin to treat ourselves with more kindness, recognizing that we're a unique expression of this amazing universe. And from this place of self-love, we naturally extend more compassion to others.

The little nudges and inklings our inner guidance sends us may not seem like much at first, but they do get louder the more we tune in to them. Developing your "sixth sense" is like paying attention to any of your physical senses. Like exercising a muscle, the more you use it the stronger it gets. You're opening a channel between your mind and your heart—the thoughts you're aware of having and the deeper perceptions that wait for your conscious mind to discover them.

Stop and Listen

Set an alarm several times a day for this quick exercise. As soon as the alarm goes off, inhale fully, then slowly exhale. Spend a full minute doing nothing but watching your breath. Go back to your breath any time a thought comes up.

Before you resume your train of thoughts or whatever you were doing, listen in! Where does your attention go? What pops into your mind? Maybe you're standing in the supplements aisle of the grocery store when you do this exercise, and you're drawn to a certain vitamin on the shelf. Or maybe an adage your grandparents used to say will come to mind and you'll suddenly know how to resolve a difficult situation. Or maybe you'll simply hear your body asking you to hydrate more.

Follow up on these nudges! You will be surprised at how often they're helpful!

The alarm you set will help you create a habit that you can practice anywhere, any time. Tune in when you're driving to work, walking your dog, preparing a meal. That moment when you first wake up in the morning is an excellent time to listen for inner guidance.

Practice Meditation

Meditation is a great way to shift your mind into alpha states where we're more receptive to inner guidance. For me, I get into alpha fast with the Hook-Up described in Chapter Three. In case you're unfamiliar with brain wave states, our brains have different gears, kind of like a car. Beta is when we're wide awake, thinking hard, maybe a bit stressed. We tend to spend most of our time in Beta.

Alpha wave state is when we're relaxed but conscious, like when we're daydreaming or just waking up. It's a calm, creative state where we're more open to intuition and inspiration. Dowsers go into alpha states while tuning into the energies of the Earth in order to locate running water.

Our love for ourselves allows us to keep showing up, to keep aiming for that bullseye of our highest potential.

Meditation doesn't have to be complicated. Think of it as taking a mini-vacation within your own mind. It's a chance to step back from the busyness of life and tune into your inner wisdom.

Find a comfortable spot where you won't be disturbed, set a timer for three minutes, and close your eyes. Then simply focus on your breath moving in and out. When thoughts come (and they will!), just notice them and return to your breath. That's it! No need to clear your mind completely or sit in a special position.

If you'd like to make it even easier, try counting your breaths from one to ten, then start over. Or put one hand on your heart to stay connected to your body. Some people enjoy gentle background music or nature sounds. I find it helpful to meditate first thing in the morning before my mind gets busy with the day's activities.

You'll know you're slipping into that receptive alpha state when your breathing naturally slows and your body feels heavy or light. Time might seem to flow differently, and you might experience a sense of spaciousness or peace. Random creative insights often pop up too. Don't worry if your mind wanders—that's totally normal! Just gently bring your attention back to your breath each time. I like to think of it as training a puppy—you wouldn't get angry at a puppy for being playful, you'd just kindly guide it back.

Once you're comfortable with this basic practice, you might want to extend the time if it feels good. Try meditating in nature or before making important decisions. It's especially helpful when feeling stressed. There's no "wrong" way to meditate. The goal isn't to achieve some perfect state of emptiness—it's simply to create space to hear your own inner wisdom more clearly.

By taking even a few minutes each day to shift into this more receptive state, you're training your brain to more easily access the peace and guidance that's always available within you. This simple practice has helped me and countless clients find our way back to center when life feels overwhelming.

Keep on Learning

Even after you've learned to listen to the guidance of your heart, you will continue to make mistakes. You will have moments of forgetting, times when you automatically fall into old habits, and situations where your triggers get the best of you. Forgive yourself and move on.

Many of us have ingrained in our minds the concept that sinning makes us bad and unlovable. This is another false belief that stands between many and the love we were created to experience.

The word "sin" has been used to make us feel bad about ourselves for far too long. But did you know that "sin" originally meant "to miss the mark?" We're always doing the best we can with what we've got. Sometimes we miss the target. Sometimes we come up short. This doesn't mean we're bad or unworthy of love.

Forming your new identity will take time and practice. Be patient with yourself.

Understanding this changes everything. Those moments when we fall short of the "mark" aren't proof of our unworthiness. They're just part of being human. Like an archer missing the bullseye, we just need a little more practice. Each "sin" is an opportunity to learn, adjust, and try again.

Allow this understanding to free you from the crushing weight of perfectionism. You don't have to get it right every time to be deserving of love. You're worthy simply because you're part of this wide, beautiful universe.

And the next time you find yourself slipping into old patterns or reacting in ways you're not proud of, take a deep breath. Remember that you're not "bad." Forgive yourself, learn what you can from the experience, and try again. This is how we grow, how we evolve, how we become more of who we're meant to be.

Our love for ourselves is the foundation that allows us to keep showing up, to keep aiming for that bullseye of our highest potential. And as we extend this compassion to ourselves, we naturally become more understanding of the people around us who are growing and learning as well.

Create Your New Identity

Now that you know you are a creator, it's time to take ownership and put those powers to work. One of the first things that you get to re-create is your identity, your beliefs about yourself. You are cherished and beloved, and it's about time you saw yourself that way!

Find a quiet, comfortable space where you can spend fifteen minutes without being disturbed.

Take a few deep breaths to ground yourself in the present moment. As you breathe, imagine roots growing from the base of your spine, anchoring you safely to the Earth.

Now, think of a time when you felt loved. This might have been a moment with a friend, a pet, or even a stranger who showed you unexpected kindness. If you can't think of a specific moment, imagine what it would feel like to be completely accepted and cared for.

As you recall or imagine this feeling, notice where you feel it in your body. Is there a warmth in your chest? A lightness in your shoulders?

Place your hand on this part of your body. Breathe into it, allowing the feeling to grow and expand.

Now, say to yourself: "I am cherished. I am beloved. I am worthy of love." Repeat this slowly three times. Really let the words sink in.

If you notice any resistance or negative self-talk arising, that's okay. Acknowledge it gently, and then return to the phrase: "I am cherished. I am beloved. I am worthy of love."

To reinforce this new identity, think of one small action you can take today to treat yourself as someone who is cherished and beloved. It might be speaking to yourself more kindly, taking a relaxing bath, or saying no to something that doesn't feel right for you.

Forming your new identity will take time and practice. Be patient with yourself. Each time you choose to see yourself as beloved, you're making progress.

You *are* worthy of love, simply because you exist. You are a unique, irreplaceable part of this universe. And you deserve to see yourself as the cherished, beloved being that you truly are.

Fill Your Life with Joy

My original intention behind writing this book was for you to cherish your life so deeply that you wouldn't mind living it all over again. That kind of life doesn't just happen though—you have to create it. It sounds like a pretty tall order during these challenging times, doesn't it?

It's worth doing though, because if you can start loving your life in the midst of all the turmoil, the whole world wins. Each of us can play a part in raising the vibration of the planet by filling our hearts to overflowing with love.

I realized that our lives can be filled with joy when I understood that everything that exists is an expression of the same universal love. Many of us call it God, All That Is, Creation, or Source. Whatever name you use, we're talking about the same thing.

Back in 2003, a research team led by Keltner and Haidt figured out what creates feelings of awe. It happens when you see something so grand or amazing that you can't wrap your mind around it. And instead of being scary, it feels wonderful! It feels like you're a tiny part of something vast and beautiful–the eternity of all that is, and there is no separation.

The first step in creating a life filled with joy is to envision it.

I felt awe when I realized that everything is All One. It started with an awareness when I went to Africa in my twenties. I learned that things I thought were so different are actually similar: my small town of 800 in upper Michigan and the small town Ajumako where I was teaching in Ghana, West Africa, each had five churches and three gas stations.

Awe came over me again when I saw the reproductive system of a male deer looking exactly like wood covered seeds from a tree in Africa. Both had a septum between two seed pods with a covering over them.

Yet again, while snorkeling in California, I was amazed how seaweed growing from the ocean floor all the way up to the shimmering sunlit surface of the water was similar to a forest on land. The beauty of it silenced my mind and blasted my heart wide open.

Hearing Michelle's story I shared earlier in this chapter showed me how real the non-physical aspects of our human lives are—we have a spiritual part that can be a positive force, like angels!

And so many other moments have given me glimpses of the amazing, interconnected web of life that we all belong to. This, for me, is what it means to live a joyful life.

Your personal wellsprings of joy will probably look a little different from mine. The key is to keep looking for them–and celebrating them!

The first step in creating a life filled with joy is to envision it. Find little pieces wherever you can, and nurture them so they grow.

Are there people in your life who inspire joy and bring out the best in you? Spend more time with them!

Can you think of a way to make your home environment more beautiful or harmonious? Make that change, however small it is, and reward yourself for the changes you make.

Listen to music that lifts your energy.

Set boundaries around your downtime.

Ask others for help when you need it.

Freely wear what makes you comfortable, and dress up when you want to.

These are small but significant ways of showing love for yourself and making your life just a little bit more joyful, one moment at a time.

You are Love

As you close this book, remember that you are love. Not just loved, but love itself. When you let yourself feel that truth in your heart, you're coming home to the very essence of who you are. And expressing that love in your life results in a tremendously fulfilling life, a life well lived!

Practice: Anchoring Joy

Joy is something you feel in your body. Your chest opens up, your shoulders drop, there's a warmth or lightness inside you. Joy doesn't have to be fleeting, and you don't have to wait for it to come to you. You can create your own joy, save it up in your body, and access it any time you need to. Here's how to anchor your joy.

First, pick a gesture you don't make often, like pressing your thumb and forefinger together.

Now bring up a joyful memory. Maybe it's holding a new baby, or finishing something you worked hard on, or a moment with someone you love. Picture it. Let yourself feel it in your body again. When the feeling is strong, do your gesture and hold it for a few seconds.

Do this ten or twelve times over the coming weeks—sometimes with memories, sometimes when joy shows up on its own. Anchor your joy when you are feeling great after a physical workout, when you are looking forward to enjoying the company of a close friend, whenever you find yourself surrounded by beauty.

Each time you practice this, your body is learning to connect that gesture with joy. The connection gets stronger every time. Soon the gesture itself will bring up those good feelings. You're not waiting for joy to find you. You're creating a way back to it whenever you choose.

PRACTICES, ACTIVITIES & EXERCISES

Chapter One

- Tapping (with sequence for releasing inherited emotional patterns)

Chapter Two

- Self-Love Assessment Quiz

Chapter Three

- Hook-Ups (for grounding and stress)

Chapter Four

- Birth Healing Meditation
- Ho'Oponopono Practice (Four Simple Phrases for Self-Forgiveness)
- Forgiveness Journaling

Chapter Five

- Breathing Awareness
- Birth Healing Meditation
- Body Movement Practices (dance, cycling, yoga)

- Bring the Light into Your Body Visualization

Chapter Six

- Emotional Awareness Journal
- Stress Release Breathing Exercise
- Progressive Muscle Relaxation
- Cross-Arm Tapping (for stress relief)
- Food and Body Awareness Diary
- Mindful Eating Practice
- Brain-Body Integration Exercises: Cross Crawl
- Body Scan Meditation

Chapter Seven

- Mirror Work
- Self-Appreciation Songs
- Daily Celebration Practice

Chapter Eight

- Candle Breath Exercise
- End-of-Day Gratitude Practice
- Heart-Opening Practices:
    » Movement to Music

    - Animal Connection
    - Singing Affirmations
    - Chest-Opening Yoga Poses

Chapter Nine

- Three-Minute Meditation Practice
- Set Multiple Daily Alarms for Mindful Check-ins
- Outdoor Sky Gazing Practice
- Inner Wisdom Listening Exercise
- New Identity Visualization

REFERENCES AND RECOMMENDED RESOURCES

Programs and Practices

Hook-Ups (in Chapter Three) was developed by Paul and Gail Dennison as part of their Brain Gym® program from Breakthroughs International.

The headache treatment in Chapter Six was developed by John Mullen, the creator of PalmajesticsTM.

Ho'oponopono is a traditional Hawaiian practice of forgiveness and reconciliation described in the book Zero Limits by Joe Vitale and Ihaleakala Hew Len.

Books I Recommend

The Anxious Generation: How the Great Rewiring of Childhood is Causing an Epidemic of Mental Illness by Jonathan Haidt

Energy Medicine by Donna Eden

Pure Human: the hidden truth of our divinity, power, and destiny by Greg Braden

Pressing RESET: Original Strength Reloaded by Tim Anderson

You Can Heal Your Life by Louise Hay

Zero Limits: The Secret Hawaiian System for Wealth, Health, Peace, and More by Joe Vitale and Ihaleakala Hew Len

Other Resources:

Paul Chek's definition of love in Chapter Two is quoted from the Aubrey Marcus Podcast #128 "The Self, God, Love, and the Soul with Paul Chek."

About the Author

Dr. Linda Ann Westman is a chiropractic doctor who brings together practical scientific understanding with spiritual insights about healing and personal growth. Linda's approach combines her expertise in brain integration and energy work with accessible, practical wisdom about how we can create joy in our daily lives. She is passionate about helping others recognize their inherent worth and teaching them how to clear the unconscious patterns that prevent them from fully loving themselves.

Linda's understanding of human potential is grounded in both clinical experience and her own journey of learning who she is as a joy-filled being capable of inspiring happiness. As a chiropractor, she has helped thousands of people from all walks of life release old patterns and transform their lives through connecting the body, mind, and spirit. In the present book, Come Home To Yourself, she shows how we can break free from limiting beliefs.

An advocate for conscious living and personal empowerment, Linda remains actively involved in her healing community, sharing her knowledge through her writing and speaking engagements. Her work demonstrates that at any stage of life, we can create lives filled with joy, purpose, and authentic self-expression.

www.ingramcontent.com/pod-product-compliance
Lightning Source LLC
LaVergne TN
LVHW100731061126
851857LV00011B/486
* 9 7 8 1 9 6 5 1 0 1 2 2 3 *